83

THE SCOTTISH COVENANTERS
1660–1688

THE SCOTTISH COVENANTERS

1660–1688

by

IAN B. COWAN

LONDON
VICTOR GOLLANCZ LTD
1976

ISBN 0 575 02105 5

Printed in Great Britain by
The Camelot Press Ltd, Southampton

To
Gillian, Susan and Ingrid

CONTENTS

PREFACE

VIEWS ABOUT THE Covenanters have oscillated between adulation and outright condemnation of the covenanting cause and its adherents. They have been seen on one hand as political extremists and as martyrs for the cause of religious freedom on the other. Such judgments in the past frequently reflected the ecclesiastical controversies of the age in which they were written, and it is only now possible to view the covenanting struggle in a more dispassionate manner. In this respect this book is a reappraisal of evidence which has been long available to historians but in the past has been selectively used to support only one viewpoint. In so far as it is a reappraisal of readily available sources, it has not been thought necessary to impede the narrative with footnotes. The sources for cited quotations appear at the end of the volume and other references will be readily found in standard works cited in the Bibliography and those to official documents under the requisite date in the published volumes of the *Register of the Privy Council*. This attempt at reinterpretation had its genesis in a revision article on the Covenanters published in the *Scottish Historical Review*, vol. xlvii (1968), 35–52, and I am grateful to the directors of the Company of Scottish History for permission to reproduce views which I advanced in that paper. My gratitude is also due to my colleagues and former students with whom I have had occasion to discuss the subject-matter, and in particular to Dr J. Kirk who read and commented upon the text. If faults and bias remain, the responsibility is mine.

IAN B. COWAN

UNIVERSITY OF GLASGOW

INTRODUCTION

RELIGIOUS PERSECUTION HAS always commanded attention and in this respect the history of the Scottish Covenanters has attracted more than an average share of popular interest. If the years following the National Covenant of 1638 and the struggle against Charles I leading to the alliance with the English parliamentarians in the Solemn League and Covenant of 1643 have not obtained the attention which they merit, the story of how, following the death of Cromwell and the restoration of Charles II in 1660, a sizeable proportion of the Scottish people took to the hills and fields and worshipped there under their own ministers is a dramatic enough tale in itself to have ensured very considerable interest. But when persecution and a ruthless harrying of the malcontents back into the fold of the established church is accompanied by killings, the history of the persecuted assumes an even greater importance.

Ostensibly the story is simple enough, involving no more than the secession from the established church of those who refused to accept change from the presbyterian system of church government, free of state interference, attained in 1638, to an episcopal system under bishops who were visibly subordinate to the civil powers. The state in turn refused to recognize a right of secession and proceeded by force to re-unite the church. In these terms little more than straightforward religious intolerance, in an age which did not recognize toleration, would have been involved. But various factors have tended to obscure these basic issues, not least of these being the ultimate presbyterian success in 1689–90, which in retrospect gave a new dimension to the history of the persecution. Issues raised at that juncture, and bitterly contested ever since, included the basic problem as to whether the presbyterian conscience represented the wishes of the majority of the Scottish people. But even if this were the case, should presbyterians, whose avowed aim in the Solemn League and Covenant was to presbyterianize England and Ireland, be allowed a foothold in

Scotland as a means to this end? If on either of these scores
action against the Covenanters was unjustified, it could nevertheless be argued that in refusing to accept state control and
royal supremacy over the church, the Covenanters were not
only religious malcontents but also enemies of the state. In
this respect, the Pentland Rising, the battle of Bothwell
Bridge and the extravagant claims thereafter of the radical
followers of Richard Cameron—the Cameronians—who declared war upon the king and his government, have conferred
apparent justification of government action designed to curb
acts of rebellion. The main stream of presbyterians, on the
other hand, neither approved nor countenanced the extremists,
yet just as anti-covenanting historians have found it convenient to concentrate on those who suffered death, since most
of those who died were undoubtedly Cameronian, so too
presbyterian historians have tended to dwell on those who in
their terms died as "martyrs" for presbyterianism and freedom
of worship.

This estimate, which remains unsullied in popular lore,
reached its height of popularity in the nineteenth century when
seceders from the established church increasingly identified
their own struggle with the Church of Scotland and the state
with that of the Covenanters. But in recent years a marked
change has taken place. Views expressed in modern works of
scholarship have alternated between outright condemnation
of the covenants and their adherents and condemnation qualified by praise for the Covenanters and their constancy under
persecution if not for their principles. The changing emphasis
from excessive adulation to denigration and oblivion is an
interesting one and appears related to changing ecclesiastical
attitudes. In earlier eras the Covenanters were liked or disliked
as opponents of state control of the church. Today they are
more likely to be seen as unreasonable men who prevented
rapprochement between episcopacy and presbyterianism from
becoming a reality.

The *via media* between adulation and denigration is hard to
determine. There is little agreed ground between the two
opposing views or between writers of different generations.
These discrepancies, moreover, are not the result of new source

material, for all important matter has been freely available since the nineteenth century. Amid these disparate views it would be easy to agree that opinions on the Covenanters must remain "a matter of temperament",[1] were it not for the fact that few historians have ever asked simple questions about who were the Covenanters and the extent to which their cause can be equated with presbyterianism.

THE SCOTTISH COVENANTERS
1660–1688

Chapter One

THE COVENANTS

ON 27 MARCH 1625, James VI, in whose person the crowns of England and of Scotland had been united since 1603, died. If to his son and heir he left an English kingdom in which rumblings against royal absolutism had already become apparent, little indication of an impending storm was evident in Scotland. Nevertheless, the danger signals were there, if only the king and his ministers had been capable of interpreting them. Far from this being the case, however, Charles I embarked upon a series of policies which eventually brought about a full-scale revolution against the authority of the crown in Scotland and in turn triggered off the Civil War in England, which was to cost the king his throne and his life.

In Scotland, opposition to the king's policies came to a head with the drawing up between 23 and 27 February of the National Covenant, which was first subscribed on 28 February in Greyfriars church, Edinburgh, by leading nobility and barons, and on 1 March by ministers and burgesses. The antecedents of this manifesto have often been discussed, and even if the degree of premeditation which lay behind the engrossing of the covenant has never been satisfactorily established, there is general agreement that constitutional opposition to the king was as important as matters of religion. Unfortunately the radical nature of this opposition and the designs and background of those who supported it have still to be fully investigated. Indeed its very presence has often been overlooked as a result of the conservative format of the covenant itself, which has led to its description as "a constitutional, and not a revolutionary document".[1] Nevertheless the emphasis laid upon measures to be taken in "free assemblies and in Parliaments"[2] is novel and serves as a preface for later demands in 1641 for a parliament free of royal influence. As further constitutional demands were foreshadowed in the covenant so was it too in matters of religion, although in this case the antecedents of this opposition are more readily ascertained.

Religious opposition arose on two scores: one arising from inherent opposition to any innovations in the form of worship and the other from deep-seated aversion to the exercise of any form of royal authority over the church. The form of worship had been established in the initial stages of the Reformation, and if for a time the retention of a prayer book or Book of Common Order had been partially necessitated by the creation of the office of reader, as a post subordinate to that of minister, that too had been abandoned at the beginning of the seventeenth century. The usages of the Church of Scotland professed to rest upon scripture and upon scripture alone, and the sacraments, which had been restricted to baptism and communion, could only be properly administered when conjoined with public preaching. As a result the keeping of holy days and festivals was banned, as were the partaking of private communion and performance of private baptism. Kneeling to receive communion and the confirmation of children was likewise forbidden. To James VI these prohibitions were a standing grievance and on his one and only return visit to his native kingdom after his accession to the English throne he had proposed to a small convention of clergy meeting at St Andrews in July 1617 that the festivals of the Christian year should be observed, private baptism and communion be permitted, confirmation be administered once more and communion should be received in a kneeling position. Objections were immediately raised to these proposals and the king had to leave Scotland without achieving his ambition.

The following year James made a further attempt, and on this occasion he had laid his plans well in advance. The General Assembly had been called to Perth in order that ministers from the north of Scotland, who were known to be more favourable to the crown proposals, might the more readily attend the assembly, while on the other hand possible opponents of the measures were excluded from the commissioners. Even with such preparation the proposals were not received with much enthusiasm, and only obtained the approval of the assembly after heated debate. The reaction of the people to these changes varied from area to area, with the question of kneeling at communion as the focal point of discontent. Accounts vary as to the extent of the disobedience to these five articles enacted at Perth, but it is obvious that it was considerable; so considerable, in fact, that James, who with some justification, could claim to know the stomach of that people, abandoned any further attempts towards liturgical innovations, including a projected prayer book, and promised that the church thereafter would be left at peace. The strength of the opposition had been greater than James had imagined and while the king had ostensibly won his point, the atmosphere created by the passing of the articles, and the widespread non-conformity with their dictates, was not conducive to ecclesiastical peace.

This peace was to be totally shattered by the introduction of a high-church policy by Charles I. However, this change did not come about immediately and the king's first actions were designed to aid the church by providing a solution to the problem of securing a permanent endowment for beneficed ministers. The major difficulty, which had perplexed statesmen and ministers alike ever since the Reformation, was in devising a plan whereby the teinds or tithes, which in many cases had become inextricably confused with temporal rents, could be separated from the latter and used to provide a permanent source of endowment for the church. By a series of acts, commencing with an Act of Revocation in 1625, Charles, if not entirely succeeding in extricating the teinds, was able to release large sums of money for the established church. But the machinery provided to effect this was, of necessity, cumbersome and slow and few churchmen felt instant gratitude towards the crown. Moreover, these actions inevitably involved the crown in difficulties with members of the nobility, who resented not only the loss of revenue from teinds but also feared that other provisions of the Act of Revocation might be implemented and that their lands too might be in jeopardy.

Other ecclesiastical developments added to the mounting opposition. In the parliament of 1633, acts relating to religious issues which had been passed in the reign of James VI were confirmed. Among them was an act of 1609 conferring upon the king the right to determine clerical vesture, and during the king's visit in 1633 contemporary English clerical vesture was worn: the rochet by bishops and the surplice by ministers. Many were offended by this gesture, and events were not helped by a further order that such dress was thenceforward to be regularly used. More far-reaching changes were to follow. These concerned the preparation of a liturgy for the Scottish church. In this project Charles himself was to take a great personal interest, and many of the ultimate innovations were to be the result of his intervention. Archbishop Laud, on the other hand, from the beginning would have preferred the English prayer book introduced in its entirety into Scotland, but had given way to representations by the Scottish bishops in favour of a distinctively Scottish book. On this issue Charles was far from happy and attempted to ensure that the new liturgy would be as close to the English mode as possible. Nevertheless, the Scottish compilers were able to ensure that some of their native tradition was incorporated in the new book. Beyond certain limits the king would not go, however, and attempts to eliminate lessons from the Apocrypha and to limit the Kalendar, were unsuccessful. Indeed, on those and other issues, the book, when finally produced in 1637, went to quite the other extreme. The Kalendar contained more saint's days than the corresponding English version, the position of the minister during communion recalled the mass, and references to ornaments were likewise liable to arouse hostility. Most damaging of all was the book's prescription, not by authority of the church, but by royal fiat; a fact which did much to ensure its condemnation whatever its theological implications.

The new book, which had been preceded by an equally controversial Code of Canons, was first used on 23 July 1637, and was the occasion of a pre-arranged tumult in St Giles cathedral. The legend of Jenny Geddes and the stool which she is said to have hurled at the minister has passed into popular currency, and, while its authenticity is more than suspect, the riot is well substantiated. Similar disturbances took place elsewhere, including Glasgow, and petitions against its use were quickly drawn up.

The disaffection produced by the introduction of the prayer

book brought to a head the dissatisfaction which had been slowly rising since 1633. The nobility, their suspicion aroused by the Act of Revocation, had further complaints on the score that Charles had of late been relying more and more on the episcopal bench in his Privy Council; a situation which had been made intolerable by the appointment of Archbishop Spottiswoode of St Andrews as chancellor. The burghs, more-over, were flinching under increased taxation, and Edinburgh in particular had cause for complaint owing to the high cost of renovating St Giles, which had become the cathedral for the newly created bishopric of Edinburgh in 1633, supplying alter-native churches for its parishioners and erecting a new parlia-ment house. All this dissatisfaction was brought to a ferment by the introduction of the prayer book and it seems likely that Charles' opponents had been awaiting such an issue as a catalyst for their various grievances. The opposition became organized with an alacrity which must have been preconceived and four committees consisting of nobility, gentry, ministers and burgesses were formed to receive petitions against current grievances. These committees sat at four different tables in Parliament House, and from this fact came to be known as the Tables.

The National Covenant was the natural outcome of this activity, in the cause of which the Tables had moved from re-ceiving petitions to issuing mandates in their own name. On ecclesiastical issues the covenant was curiously and almost certainly deliberately cautious. But while it can be maintained (since episcopal government is not condemned nor the five articles of Perth specifically rejected) that the Covenanters only intended to sweep away recent innovations which had not been approved by statute law, the emphasis upon acts of "lawful general assemblies"[3] suggests that there had been some unlawful ones, and later in the year all assemblies since 1606 were to be so regarded. The Earl of Rothes, moreover, was quite insistent that the reason for passing the Perth articles was no longer valid and "the reason of the law was the force of the law".[4] Though some subscribed the covenant with a reserva-tion in favour of episcopacy and the five articles, they had little doubt as to the covenant's true intent.

These intentions quickly came to the fore and whereas initial demands were for the withdrawal of the prayer book and the canons, coupled with a request for the removal of the bishops from the Privy Council, fresh demands for the abolition of the Court of High Commission, the summoning of a free parliament and a general assembly soon followed. The idea of a free general assembly did not appeal to Charles but he was persuaded that his commissioner, the Marquis of Hamilton, would be able to keep discussion within reasonable limits and in the last resort would be able to dissolve the assembly. In this hope, however, Charles was to be sadly disappointed.

The assembly met at Glasgow on 21 November 1638, and from the outset it became apparent it was not going to be easily controlled. The anti-episcopal element had used their influence not only to exclude their opponents but also had strengthened their own party by introducing as commissioners elders elected by presbyteries. It soon became obvious that the bishops, unpopular for their share in the making of the prayer book and also for the political power which they had wielded, were to be the subject of an attack in which few hands would be raised to defend them. The charges levelled at the bishops were varied, and in certain respects of more than doubtful authenticity. Arminianism, popery, the inbringing of the prayer book and the canons, immorality and simony were amongst the accusations made, and eventually accepted by the assembly. In vain Charles' commissioner tried to dissolve the assembly on the grounds that it was not competent to deal with such matters, but his objections were rejected, and when the commissioner withdrew the assembly continued with its business. Nevertheless, while the bishops had been condemned, difficulties arose over the condemnation of the office of bishop, and it was only after the clerk to the assembly, Johnston of Warriston, produced the records of previous assemblies in which episcopacy had already been condemned that the final decision was taken that episcopacy should be removed and abjured.

In this manner the general assembly re-asserted its claim to supreme authority over the church. This claim had been evident from the earliest days of the Scottish Reformation,

final authority in a number of ecclesiastical issues being reserved by the reformers in their book of reformation for a
supreme council or assembly "of the Universal Kirk gathered
within the realm".[5] This principle had been reinforced by the
Second Book of Discipline in 1578 and the subsequent advocation by Andrew Melville of a fully-fledged presbyterian programme. Bishops who in the early days of the Reformed
Church had been allowed to function within its conciliar
framework were to be abolished and the courts of the church
ranging from the general assembly through synods and presbyteries to the kirk session were to hold all ecclesiastical power
in their hands. In theory the authority of the crown was restricted to temporal matters, but in practice many may have
continued to regard the godly prince as acting in concert with
the church in the creation of a godly commonwealth. This was
certainly the role cast for the sovereign by the first generation
of reformers, but it is equally clear that they would not have
accepted the sovereign as head of the church. On the other
hand James VI, if unwilling to assume such a title, firmly
believed that the sovereign should control the church. This
was most easily accomplished through bishops and from 1600
onwards James not only appointed bishops by royal prerogative
but gradually enlarged their sphere of authority to the point
at which they were no longer answerable to the courts of the
church. This process was completed in 1612 when three
Scottish bishops were consecrated in England according to the
English ordinal, and on their return to Scotland consecrated
their fellow bishops. In this matter James' triumph has often
been held to be complete, but this may be queried. His insistence on the five articles and the craven attitude adopted by
the bishops to his proposals may not only have discredited
the bishops as individuals but may also have undermined
the structure of episcopal organization which he had so
laboriously erected. King James, every bit as much as his
son, may have initiated the process which led to the Glasgow
assembly.

This assembly which carried the ecclesiastical revolution to
fruition was demonstrably packed. Had it consisted solely of
ministers its decisions might have been very different; but it

can be argued that its very irregularities helped it come nearer
to the will of the majority of the people than had any other of
the equally unrepresentative assemblies since 1606. How far
this is true must remain a matter of debate; and if the majority
may not have wished the condemnation of the office of bishop
few had any love for the bishops of Charles I, and the five
articles were widely detested especially among the laity. To all
but the most ardent supporters of episcopacy, this condemnation must have appeared a matter of little regret and a small
price for the king's political opponents to pay for further
support. That support was considerable, and to argue that a
majority in the assembly disregarded "parliament, king and
country alike"[6] is a doubtful thesis, for it can be equally
asserted that this triumph of the laity in ecclesiastical matters
mirrored the general will, and in 1640 parliament set its seal
of approval upon the assembly's actions. The king alone was
defied and even if the solidarity of the covenant was slightly
disturbed by the deposition of ministers hostile to the abolition
of episcopacy and the alienation also of others committed to
that cause, the king's alternative covenant attracted few sub-
scriptions and the example of Huntly in holding aloof was
not generally followed. In the north more opposition to
the covenant was certainly forthcoming than in the south,
but if Aberdeen was decidedly anti-covenanting there is
evidence of covenanting support in Easter Ross, Caithness
and Strathnaver, and politically, if not religiously, supporters
of the covenant were soon to be found in other parts of the
Highlands.

At this stage the opposition clearly embraced two revolutionary causes: that of presbytery and that of the establishment
of a constitutional monarchy, by which the king's opponents
probably meant that Charles should defer to the wishes of the
estates of the realm. Montrose, no lover of bishops, embraced
these two views, which at this juncture remained the ideals of
the majority of a convenanted nation. These ideals proved to
be incompatible and most authorities are agreed that the
prime cause of division lay in the basic inconsistency of the
covenant whereby an attempt was made to defend the person
and authority of the king while at the same time promoting

policies contrary to his interest. The interpretation which came to be given to these policies and the realization that a "balanced constitution"[7] could not be achieved led Montrose in particular to become increasingly alarmed as royal authority was assailed beyond the point which he deemed desirable. This awareness and the activities of the Earl of Argyll in turning these developments to his advantage led to the Cumbernauld Bond of August 1640, in which an appeal was made to "the public ends" of the covenant against "the particular and indirect practicking of a few".[8] Sympathy with this viewpoint was to grow as more of the nobility realized they had unleashed a force which they could not control. Nevertheless support for presbyterianism was sufficiently widespread and distrust in Charles was so deep-rooted that, although a narrow majority in council was prepared to trust the king, the view of the assembly and of other council members prevailed.

In the meantime Charles, who had tried in 1639 to coerce his opponents by military intervention but in the face of a superior Scottish army had instead been forced by the Pacification of Berwick to promise to call a free assembly and free parliament, found his cause going from bad to worse. The general assembly when it met in Edinburgh on 12 August 1639 had proceeded not only to ratify the actions of the Glasgow assembly but also obtained from the Privy Council an act making subscription to the covenant universally compulsory. Charles through his commissioner had ratified this action but had refused to do likewise when parliament meeting a little later threatened to encompass in the state what had been effected in the church, since it not only confirmed the actions of the assembly and the Privy Council but went on to claim a voice in the appointment of offices of state, and approved a proposal to recast the mode of choosing the lords of the articles which, if effected, would have freed parliament from royal domination. In the event, Charles was forced to summon his English parliament in the hope that their natural antipathy towards the Scots would lead to a substantial grant towards the cost of waging another campaign. This was not to be and Charles was forced to dissolve the Short Parliament without solving his difficulties. As a result the king had to face the second Scottish invasion of England with ill-equipped and ill-trained levies. Not surprisingly his venture in the Second Bishops' War was singularly unsuccessful, and, as the Scots would not leave northern England without a financial settlement, yet another parliament had to be summoned. With the calling of the Long Parliament a chain of events was initiated which culminated in the outbreak of civil war in August 1642.

The initial engagements of the Civil War having proved inconclusive both king and parliament sought assistance from the Scots. A narrow majority in council was prepared to trust the king, but support for presbyterianism was sufficiently widespread and distrust of Charles so deep-rooted that the view of the assembly and of other council members that parliament should gain their support prevailed and was given shape in the Solemn League and Covenant of August–September 1643. The reasons for such a compact according to the covenant lay in the "conspiracies, attempts and practices of the enemies of God against the true religion" and stated the aims of the covenant as "the preservation of the reformed religion in the Church of Scotland" and "the reformation of religion in the kingdoms of England and Ireland".[9] Such aims not unnaturally gave to the covenant the aspect of a presbyterian crusade. To some, the covenant certainly became such a symbol and subsequent commentators have invariably condemned it in this respect. In consequence it has been called "a most wantonly aggressive measure" and if others have been less outspoken there has been general disapproval of the concept of divine right of presbytery to which the solemn league gave articulate expression.[10] It is far from certain, however, that this was the covenant's main attraction to the Scots who, no less than the English parliamentarians, saw in this alliance the opportunity of perpetuating their own political power by ensuring that the king's authority was equally diminished in both kingdoms.

The solemn league by extending the claims of presbyterianism and establishing an alliance with the English parliament against the king certainly clarified the incongruity of the earlier situation. To some, including Montrose, this was a far from popular move and Robert Baillie writing of the opposition to it attributed to "God's great mercy" the fact that reaction had not been more serious.[11] The divisions which took place at this time are difficult to pin-point and they may have been overstressed. The rising of Montrose in 1644-5 was not widely supported, little help being forthcoming from southern Scotland, and even in the north the covenant had its supporters. Montrose's army was bound together by divergent interests, not least of which was enmity to the clan Campbell and its leader Argyll rather than to the covenant. Defeat was inevitable and the importance of the rising is not in the extent of support which the Malignants (i.e. opponents of the covenant) comanded, but rather in the irreparable damage which they inflicted on the convenanting cause. Victory when it came at Philiphaugh near Selkirk in September 1645 "was too late to undo the damage to the prestige of the covenanters", whose chances of implementing the solemn league were brought to an end by the withdrawal of much of their army from England and the consequent loss of "military authority on which they had counted to maintain their moral dominance over their allies".[12]

The Scots had, however, achieved the downfall of the king, playing a decisive part in his defeat at Marston Moor in July 1644. This had been followed by a further reverse at Naseby in June 1645 after which the Scots looked forward to the fruits of victory only to have these denied to them by their own inability to deal with Montrose in a quick enough manner and also by the rising importance of the model army in which independency, not presbyterianism, was to be the dominant force. By 1646 the Scots were conscious that their cause was in jeopardy and the king himself showed keen awareness of the situation when he chose in May of that year to surrender to the Scottish army rather than its English counterpart. Charles refused to implement the covenant and offered instead to introduce presbyterianism into England for three years, but not only was such a compromise unacceptable to many Scots but even those who would have been prepared to temporize must have seen that the Scots could not effectively support the king at this juncture. In consequence, virtue was made out of necessity; the king was surrendered to parliament which in turn promised to settle the arrears due to the Scottish army.

Thereafter the fate of the king rested entirely upon the result of the struggle between parliament and the army.

With Charles' surrender and the realization by many in Scotland that the establishment of presbyterianism as envisaged by the solemn league was becoming more remote, new attitudes began to appear on how the divergent interests of the two covenants could be reconciled. To the nobility the safeguarding of the king and (by implication) of their own interests became the prime consideration; while to the assembly the establishment of presbyterianism was paramount. The Engagement of December 1647 whereby the Scots undertook to intervene on Charles' behalf in return for a promise to establish presbyterianism in England for a trial period of three years was a further attempt to reconcile these two interests, but in so far as the king was not personally to become covenanted, greater emphasis was laid on the first of these desires. To a general assembly, which earlier that year had approved as a basis of presbyterian unity the Confession of Faith, Larger and Shorter Catechisms, Directory of Worship and Form of Church Government which had been prepared by the Westminster assembly at which the Scots had been represented by eight commissioners since August 1643, such a compromise was totally unacceptable. Even though the Engagement did not abandon the solemn league, which was to be confirmed by act of parliament in both countries, and even if the form of church government to be allowed to the English after three years of presbyterianism was, with its emphasis upon its form as being that "most agreeable to the word of God"[13] (with its echoes of the solemn league), subject to only one interpretation by most Scots, the opposition in the assembly was implacable. The Engagement was a compromise and as such it was unacceptable to the majority in the assembly who now believed that as presbyterianism was *juris divini* its establishment could not be a matter for negotiation. By bringing this crisis to a head, and producing the first formal demonstration that theocracy might be more dangerous than autocracy, the Engagement shattered the unity of the covenanting movement. Thereafter a majority of the nation opposed the party which preferred a presbyterian theocracy to the defence of kingship.

For the time being, however, the minority prevailed. Lack of unity among their opponents, the defeat of the army of the Engagers at Preston in August 1648 and the ensuing support of Cromwell for a party with which he disagreed on almost every issue except their mutual dislike of the Engagement, have all been recognized as reasons for the rule of a "clerical oligarchy" which lasted from 1648 until the battle of Dunbar in 1650.[14] This régime found its fullest expression in that "Gideon-like measure"[15] the Act of Classes (January 1649) which debarred Engagers and all other Malignants who might be adjudged as plotters against the covenant, promoters of the Engagement and supporters of Montrose from public office for varying terms. Its censorious nature is illustrated by the debarment from office of those: "who being members of judicatories, clerkis and persons in publict trust as aforsaid are given to uncleannesse, brybery, swearing, drunkennesse, or deceiving, or are otherwise openlie profane and grosslie scandalous in their conversatioun or who neglect the worship of God in thair families".[16] Nevertheless, despite the overt control exercised by the ministers who were further strengthened and released from dependence on the nobility and gentry by the abolition of ecclesiastical patronage on 9 March 1649, it is far from certain that final power lay with the churchmen. The nobility, with the exception of a few notables such as Argyll, Cassillis, Eglinton and Loudon, were dispossessed of influence, as were many of the influential gentry, but beneath these classes lay a new stratum of lay society—small lairds and tenant farmers—whose wishes could be expressed as elders in presbyteries and in the assembly. In this respect the growth of the practice of keeping elders in office for life takes on a new significance, and in association with the Act of Classes may be seen as a means of indefinitely extending the political power of the godly minority.

If the aim of this régime was to produce a more God-fearing realm, it also remained their intention to enforce the covenant, but if the theory that its establishment could not be a matter of negotiation had been sound practical politics at the time of the Engagement, the execution of Charles I on 30 January 1649 dictated otherwise thereafter. Charles II was proclaimed king but his acceptance was only conditional on his acceptance of the covenants, a stipulation which Charles found impossible to avoid. The acceptance of Charles made war with Cromwell inevitable, but no one except those acceptable to the faithful were to be allowed to fight. The Act of Classes was to be rigidly enforced and in the very face of the enemy the Scots army was purged of unsatisfactory elements. If this did not entirely contribute to the rout of the Scots at Dunbar on 3 September 1650, neither did it endear the oligarchy to those who had suffered under it. Defeat produced an immediate reaction in favour of more moderate opinion within the country. In the face of this the extremists initially proved to be intractable and produced in October 1650 the Remonstrance in which they rejected the king until he provided evidence of his sincerity, contended that the Act of Classes had not been strict enough in its provisions and declared "the grate and mother sin of this nation . . . to be the backslydinge breache of covenant".[17] The moderates held the upper hand, however, and an alliance constructed between the Malignants and the Engagers was forwarded by the condemnation of the Remonstrance by the Committee of Estates on 25 November 1650. Further support was forthcoming in the first public resolution of the Commission of Assembly in December 1650—which gave its adherents their new name of Resolutioners. In consequence Engagers and even supporters of Montrose, who had been hanged after an abortive royal coup in April, were allowed to enter public service again; the Remonstrants were crushed at Hamilton and unity was again in sight.

The coronation of Charles II at Scone on 1 January 1651 was symbolic of this new unity, and the second public resolution of the Commission of Assembly and the repeal of the Act of Classes in June 1651 added to this new spirit of co-operation. Even before these events, however, Cromwell had intervened and gradually set about conquering the country. His northern advance allowed the Scots army to slip into England but to no avail and the disaster which had threatened them throughout the year finally overtook them at Worcester on 3 September 1651. This defeat, and the subsequent flight of Charles II to the continent, meant subjugation for Scotland and until the

Restoration in 1660 the Scots were to be ruled by an authoritarian régime, which, while hated, did nevertheless make a genuine and not always unsuccessful attempt to solve the problems of Scotland.

The character of the struggle changed at this juncture for whereas until Dunbar military success or defeat in the field had been reflected in a change of power in the church and state, this ceased to be true after the defeat of the Resolutioners at Worcester. Nevertheless, only a military occupation which limited the pretensions of both parties allowed the Remonstrants some semblance of continuing secular authority thereafter. From 1651 they were to become more like a secession church than an active political force, for in July of that year Samuel Rutherford, minister of Anwoth, and 21 fellow ministers had declared the assembly in which they were then present to be unconstitutional and invalid. After Worcester those Protesters as heirs to the Remonstrants completed their secession by declaring that they could not recognize a commission of the church emanating from a pretended assembly, and restored the commission appointed by the preceding assembly in as much as it included persons of their own number, with no limit to the duration of their power. The 1652 assembly was likewise declared invalid and as a contemporary pamphlet observed of the Protesters: "The Churchmen were thus able to assert against their 'dissenting brethren' that they had set themselves down as a Commission which . . . may be a perpetual court, seeing they allege the continuance of their power till the new free and lawful general assembly, and none such can be had so long as they please to protest against it."[18] The Protesters maintained this attitude, however, and in 1653 the rival assemblies whose meeting places in St Giles were separated only by a partition were dispersed by the military. Conferences were held from time to time to try to heal the rupture, but, since the Protesters were adamant that only purged assemblies would be acceptable lest the godly were outvoted, these negotiations came to nought.

The support enjoyed by the respective parties is difficult to assess. Arguments over the number of adherents have tended to revolve around the ministry, whereas support amongst the laity is the more critical issue. Support amongst the ministers for the Protesters was relatively small. The Resolutioners claimed 750 out of 900 parish ministers, but this is not to say that the Protesters could have mustered 150 committed supporters since vacancies and waverers must have further depleted this number. Nevertheless, some 113 ministers drawn mainly from the central belt and south-eastern counties with a fairly strong outpost in Aberdeenshire actively supported their cause. If they were numerically weaker than their opponents it must be equally remembered that of the 750 ministers claimed by the Resolutioners only 600 actually adhered to the Resolutions. Of these all but 40 were to conform to episcopacy in 1661. The other 150 can be classed as waverers and it was from their numbers that a large number of non-conformists were to appear. All in all some 300 ministers, or one third of the ministry, seem to have been dissatisfied with the Erastian nature of the Resolutioner settlement, and, if only one third of this number were prepared to go as far as the Protesters and enter into what was in effect a schismatic church, this feeling of loyalty to an undivided church was not to withstand the changes of the Restoration period during the course of which one third of the total ministry chose to leave the established church. Sympathy, if not active support, for the Protesters even amongst the ministers was a significant feature of the Cromwellian interlude. When to this is added a very considerable, but largely incalculable, support amongst the laity the strength of the Protesters must not be under-rated. Any weakness, moreover, was counterbalanced by the favour shown to them as anti-royalists by Cromwell. That favour led to the intrusion of their ministers in certain areas, but, as Resolution synods can be found re-admitting former Malignants, little change in the balance of power probably occurred in that direction during the Cromwellian period.

The struggle between Resolutioners and Protesters dominates the period 1651–60, but, in so far as it often hinged either on a practical bid to obtain control of the church by one or other of the factions, the minutiae of the arguments used in attempts to attain this end tend to obscure the very real bond of agreement which continued to bind both parties. The Resolutioners remained as staunchly presbyterian as their opponents, and, if less committed to the solemn league or even to the Engagement as years went past, certainly never envisaged anything other than the continuance of presbyterianism in Scotland and consistently worked towards the revival of general assemblies without which they believed the system was impotent. Even the covenant was not abandoned but its implementation was no longer to be enforced, but to become a matter of negotiation. Not all within the Resolutioner party would have agreed with this qualification, however, and within the ranks of the Resolutioners there were already signs of the breach which was to open in 1661. For whereas some were prepared to treat with an Erastian ruler in Cromwell, others had scruples and were decidedly anti-Erastian in their views. Thus one of their leading members, Robert Blair, was unfavourable to the mission of James Sharp as Resolutioner spokesman to an Erastian ruler in August 1656 and had joined with others, including ministers from Fife, in regretting censures passed on Protesters who shared this viewpoint. Even within that party, which was much more single-minded on the sanctity of the covenant, divergence on this issue could be marked, for, whereas some such as Patrick Gillespie and John Livingstone were willing to negotiate with the state and would have accepted a commission of 1655 putting the church under the Protesters, Johnston of Warriston and James Guthrie rejected it for its "Erastian character".[19] The point at which willingness to compromise with the state in its relationship to the church became Erastianism was a matter of fine distinction and admittedly often arbitrarily determined by those who were currently out of favour when they were seeking a convenient term of abuse for attacking opponents who enjoyed overt state support. Nevertheless, despite a gradual acceptance, even by Warriston who had initially rigidly maintained the doctrine of the "two kingdoms", of the need for some such co-operation, almost all, whether Resolutioners or Protesters, had a point beyond which they would not normally venture. In their negotiations with Cromwell both factions overstepped this mark in an effort to gain permanent advantage over the other. Blinded by their own in-fighting, the death of the Protector on

B

3 September 1658 left both parties totally unprepared to meet a situation in which battle was to be joined not on the issue of which of the conflicting presbyterian parties was to emerge as victor, but as to whether presbyterianism in any meaningful form was to survive at all.

Chapter Two

THE RESTORATION SETTLEMENT

FOLLOWING THE DEATH of Cromwell both Protesters and Resolutioners attempted to insinuate themselves with Cromwell's successor as Protector, his son Richard. To this end both parties sought friends in England and the Resolutioners despatched James Sharp, minister of Crail in Fife, who had successfully interceded on their behalf in 1656 in the hope that once again he might counter the influence of Johnston of Warriston who as a member of Cromwell's upper house was able to exert influence on behalf of the Protesters. At first Sharp appears to have achieved very little, spending much of his time in an endless succession of interviews, whereas Warriston backed up in parliament by the Marquis of Argyll was enjoying evident success in supporting a Bill of Union which would include a clause "for confirmation of the liberties of all Church Judicatures and Assemblies before the year 1650".[1] By this blatant piece of political opportunism the Protesters hoped to perpetuate their own dominance in civil and ecclesiastical matters, but although the Resolutioners recognized this they felt increasingly powerless to impede it. In fact the Protester success was more apparent than real, and Sharp who was less despondent than some of his fellow Resolutioners did note that parliament had not "fallen upon the way of beginning to do anything",[2] whereas his own interviews, and particularly those with the earls of Lauderdale and Crawford who were imprisoned at Windsor, had prepared the way for more meaningful discussions in the future. For the time being, however, Sharp was powerless and with the deposition of the Protector and the assumption of control by a new council of state, over which Warriston frequently presided, his mission was terminated by an order of 29 June 1659 to return to Scotland, resume his pastoral and private duties and refrain from meddling, directly or indirectly, with public affairs.

There matters rested until November when after a period of unsettled military rule the Scottish commander, General Monck, decided to break the deadlock by restoring the freedom of parliament. The possibility of the re-admission of excluded members with presbyterian and monarchical sympathies brought fresh hope to the Resolutioners as such a programme was in full accord with their own aspirations. Of this Monck was not unaware and he actively sought the assistance of prominent Resolutioner ministers. Foremost amongst these was James Sharp whose diplomatic ability had already been recognized and who was now summoned by Monck to help him prepare a Declaration of Intent, which was circulated throughout the country before the general crossed the border at Coldstream on 1 January 1660. London was reached on 3 February but restoration of the monarchy was not to be effected until May, and the intervening months proved to be decisive for the future of presbyterianism in both England and Scotland.

The importance of negotiation was recognized at an early stage and both Monck and the Resolutioners were agreed that James Sharp was well qualified for such a task. On 15 January 1660 Monck had requested Sharp "to undertake a winter journey and to come to him to London with as much convenient speed as your occasions can possible permit".[3] The reasons for the summons were not to be divulged until after his arrival. But even before this date Sharp had been commissioned by some of his Resolutioner brethren, including Robert Douglas and David Dickson, to proceed to London in order to "give information to others of the state of this Church".[4] Sharp arrived in London on 13 February and negotiations began almost at once.

The early stages of these negotiations with Monck and others were mainly concerned with attempts to further the cause of presbyterianism in England. To this end Sharp was active in persuading Monck to restore the excluded members to parliament, and this was effected on 21 February accompanied by a plea from Monck for "presbyterian government not rigid".[5] At this stage Sharp was certainly regarded as a staunch presbyterian who was seemingly unconcerned with Monck's hint that presbyterianism might be thought too intractable. Douglas, on the other hand, foresaw the danger and wrote to Monck urging that presbyterianism should not be rejected "because of the rigid miscarriages of some whose irregular actings have been hateful to true presbyterians".[6] The fear that moderate presbyterians might be discredited by the excesses of the more radical was to be quickly realized in England, for, although the presence of the excluded members ensured statutory recognition for the Confession of Faith and even republication of the Solemn League and Covenant, these expiring efforts of English presbyterianism commanded little popular support.

As his correspondence reveals, Sharp clearly foresaw that with the dissolution of the Long Parliament these enactments would be swept away by the newly-elected parliament which predictably and unequivocally declared for monarchy in the state and episcopacy in the church. For some time Sharp appears to have hoped that a moderate episcopal settlement might be possible, but in this respect also Sharp's hopes were to be overtaken by events. Such attempts that he did make to follow his instructions and secure the covenant were in vain, and, after a meeting in London with Lauderdale and ten city ministers at which it was "agreed upon the necessity of endeavouring to bring in the king upon Covenant terms", Sharp, nevertheless, wrote on 5 April 1660: "I see not full ground of hope, that Covenant terms will be rigidly stuck to"; and in another letter of the same month: "I fear the interest of the Solemn League and Covenant shall be neglected".[7] Those doubts were not shared by the Resolutioners in Scotland many of whom, including Douglas, pinned their hopes on the restoration of a covenanted king. Even after the king's unconditional return in May 1660 the Resolutioners were still confident of a settlement in line with the Solemn League and Covenant in both England and Scotland. Hopes of presbyterian unity were still alive as late as 7 June when the Edinburgh ministers instructed Sharp to inform English ministers that their Scottish brethren believed that with God's guidance it surely would not be too difficult to persuade the king to prevent an episcopal settlement. Events thereafter persuaded them otherwise, but by then Charles II was unconditionally restored and the initiative, which might have been theirs before the Restoration, was lost.

In this respect the culpability of Sharp for this state of affairs is open to question. Some success attended his initial efforts to promote the cause of the covenant, but his ability to influence events in that direction vanished with the dissolution of the Long Parliament on 16 March. Thereafter, Sharp could only observe and concur in the course of events in England. These changes he purported to report to his fellow Resolutioners, but his letters were seldom as forthcoming as they might have been and at other times were downright misleading. As late as 7 April 1660 he could still write: "We may look for a settlement upon the grounds of the Covenant and thereby a foundation laid for security against the prelaticall and phanaticky assaults."[8] At this stage he was fully aware that such a conclusion was unlikely, but only in the course of May and June when this was certain did the truth begin to emerge. Caution and false optimism may have been Sharp's failing, but it seems more likely that he told the Resolutioners what they wanted to hear in order to maintain his own position as their spokesman. Such an attitude would also explain his reluctance to have any of the other Resolutioner ministers join him in England. This on the specious argument that the presbyterian cause was well represented in his hands and those of other Scots nobles, such as Crawford and Lauderdale, who were retained as Scottish representatives in London after their release from captivity. But they too were to prove doubtful friends to the cause of the covenant and presbyterianism, as it became increasingly obvious that whatever loyalties remained to either or both these causes would always remain subordinate to the restoration of their own political fortune.

Despite these drawbacks, the presbyterian cause before the restoration of the king was not entirely hopeless. If presbyterianism, with or without the covenant, had been made a condition of Charles' restoration to his Scottish kingdom, at least the lesser of these two ends might have been achieved. In this respect, however, the Scots suffered from two serious disadvantages. One, which stemmed from the Cromwellian union, was the absence of any of the normal constitutional organs of government through which any such negotiations could have been conducted, and the other was the advice of Sharp to leave such matters until after the restoration of the king. Caution exuded from Sharp. "For Gods sake," he wrote, "take care that our people keep themselves quiet and wait till the Lord give a fitt opportunity."[9] His prediction that the Scottish cause would suffer from the maintenance of "rigid presbyterianism" was accompanied by warnings that a similar loss of advantage would result if Scotland was thought in any way unenthusiastic about the restoration of the monarchy. The Protesters, to whom the return of the king was "a matter of terrour",[10] were certainly not zealous for a restoration, and rumours that the Resolutioners were like-minded would inevitably damage their cause. In all this Sharp may have been genuinely motivated by a desire to ensure that presbyterians in general should not have prejudice created against them by a small minority who had expressed opposition to the king's restoration. Whatever the motivation, however, the effect of this advice, coupled with the hope that acceptance of the covenant would allow a joint settlement for both kingdoms, created a delay which was to prove fatal to presbyterian interests. At a later date some were to suggest that his defection had gone much further and Douglas eventually alleged that Sharp had utilized interviews with Charles at Breda to prove that "he was a great enemy to the Presbyterian interest",[11] but of this, and other similar allegations, there is no positive proof. He was, however, increasingly regarded as a faithful servant of the crown, and Lauderdale informed Charles that "God hath made him [Sharp] as happy ane instrument in your service all along as any I know of his country".[12] Sharp clearly enjoyed this role and this may increasingly have led him to promote policies which he would otherwise have rejected. Be this as it may, wittingly or unwittingly, Sharp paved the way for an episcopal settlement in Scotland.

The realization that episcopacy might threaten presbyterian government in the Church of Scotland came very slowly to the Resolutioners. Their concern with their fellow presbyterians in England coupled with an almost total collapse in the fortunes of the Protesters had totally blinded them to such a possibility. Assurances by Sharp to the effect that he had "found his Majesty resolved to restore the kingdom to its former civil liberties, and to preserve the settled government of our church"[13] may have been capable of several interpretations but for some time they continued to be accepted at their face value. Overtures by the Protesters for concerted action between themselves and the Resolutioners over the rise of episcopacy in England were rejected out of hand by the latter who regarded the move by their rivals as opportunist and solely designed to prop up their own tottering position. This may well have been the case, but in fact the Resolutioners at this juncture were as much in need of allies as their rivals.

The opportunity for co-operation was soon to pass. On 8 July Argyll, who had gone to London to seek an audience of the king, was seized and sent to the Tower. Six days later two other prominent Protesters, Sir James Stewart, Lord Provost of Edinburgh, and Sir John Chiesley of Carsewell were arrested in Scotland, but Johnston of Warriston managed to elude capture by escaping to the continent where he was eventually apprehended and returned for execution in 1663. On 23 August, James Guthrie, minister of Stirling, and other members of the Protesters' party were arrested at what was deemed to be an illegal meeting in Edinburgh. The power of the Protesters which had steadily waned since Monck marched south seemed totally at an end and their policies were certainly not to prevail. In their extremity the Resolutioners softened somewhat in their attitude to their fallen rivals. Douglas wrote to Sharp that they were "to be pitied rather than invyed", while Sharp himself claimed that he had suggested to the king at Breda that "pity and pardon may be their measure".[14] For some at least there was to be neither pity nor pardon. Argyll, who had been conveyed to Edinburgh for trial on charges of treason, was executed on 27 May 1661 and was followed to the scaffold on 1 June by Guthrie and Lieutenant William Govan, a member of the Remonstrant army who had defected to the Cromwellian army, but whose real crime was that of having played a minor part in the execution of Charles I. These executions were the culmination of an intensive campaign which had become more severe after the arrest of Guthrie and his companions on 23 August 1660. On the following day the Committee of Estates issued a proclamation against unlawful meetings and seditious papers. Further proclamations were issued in September against Samuel Rutherford's *"Lex Rex"*[15] and also against all seditious railers and slanderers and against all unlawful convocations of the lieges. By the end of the year the Protesters had been sufficiently cowed to allow re-appraisal of the position of the Resolutioners.

By this period the Resolutioners were also beset by difficulties. The proclivity of the nobility had begun to veer towards episcopacy if for no better reason than as Sharp discovered "to bring our Church Government to a subordination to the Civill power".[16] The nobility and other great landowners from the Engagement onwards had paid a steep price for their hostility to royal autocracy, and were not prepared to do so again. If the crown wished support in curbing the pretensions of the church that support would almost certainly be forthcoming. On top of these practical difficulties the Resolutioners had also to contend with rumours that ministers in Scotland were still dissatisfied that the king had not been brought back on covenant terms, and were prepared to rise in arms to attain that end. Douglas hastily refuted the charge and boldly asserted that "such a matter is far from their thought and farther from their acting".[17] Such rumours, however untrue, certainly delayed the withdrawal of English garrisons and troops, a fact in itself which was not conducive to resolute action by those who urged an early settlement of the affairs of the church.

Such a settlement had in fact to await the re-constitution of the civil organs of government, and, although this was perhaps inevitable, it was again to place the church at a serious disadvantage in relation to the state. Shortly after his return, Charles nominated the Earl of Middleton as his commissioner to parliament and at the same time appointed as members of the Privy Council, Glencairn as chancellor, Lauderdale as secretary, Rothes as president of the council and Crawford as treasurer. The Committee of Estates nominated by parliament in 1651 was to reconvene in Edinburgh on 23 August

1660 and was to form a provisional government until parliament met. In such a manner the civil administration was quickly and efficiently revived, but no corresponding steps were taken to revive ecclesiastical administration through the calling of a General Assembly of the church.

The decision not to call an assembly was not for want of urging. Douglas and other Resolutioner ministers believed that a suitable compromise between church and state could be achieved if an assembly met. A new assembly would be preferred, but if the king cared to recall the 1653 assembly this would be acceptable. Assurances would be given that future assemblies would not interfere in civil matters and if the king called an assembly it would be seen how consistent presbytery was with monarchy. All they desired was that parliament should in no way prejudice the government of the established church, and that an assembly should be called as soon as possible. Opinions have varied as to whether an assembly was practical at this juncture and it has been argued that had an assembly been allowed to meet, the Resolutioners would have ejected the Protesters and in these circumstances it would inevitably have broken up in disorder. This may be true but assemblies in the past had proved adept in excluding their opponents beforehand and in any case after the arrest of Guthrie and his associates total disruption of an assembly was highly unlikely. An assembly was not held for the simple reason that whereas Douglas and his associates saw an assembly as a means of perpetuating the presbyterian settlement, this lesson was not lost on Charles and Sharp who claimed that such a gathering must await the settlement of civil government. By this time it seems fairly certain that Sharp had been converted to, or was at least contemplating accepting, the idea of a moderate episcopate as a solution to the problem of church-state relations. So too Lauderdale, who had hoped to find a solution compatible with the power of the king, but likewise settled for royal autocracy and a moderate episcopacy. If this was the case at this juncture both Lauderdale and Sharp were guilty of the grossest deception in a royal letter addressed to Douglas and the presbytery of Edinburgh. Subscribed by Lauderdale on 10 August 1660, this was carried north by

Sharp who reported its contents to a meeting of Edinburgh ministers on Saturday 1 September. The contents of the letter which were received with joy assured its hearers that the king had resolved to "protect and preserve the government of the Church of Scotland, as it is settled by law, without violation".[18] After all their fears, it was little wonder that Sharp was heartily thanked for his work "for the success whereof the brethren blessed the Lord."[19]

The hopes raised by this letter were quickly dashed. Lauderdale again informed Douglas on 23 October that the king intended to call an assembly and that the necessary proclamation had been drawn up, but nothing materialized. When parliament finally met on 1 January 1661 the real truth was quickly revealed as one act after another hit at the very fabric of the presbyterian establishment. Among other acts it framed an oath of allegiance, which any person might be obliged to swear, acknowledging the absolute supremacy of the king; forbade the covenant to be renewed, and appointed 29 May to be kept as a holiday in memory of the Restoration. The final blow to presbyterian hopes fell on 28 March when the Recissory Act annulled all legislation since 1633. It was accompanied by an act which declared that the king would maintain the church's doctrine and worship as "it was established within this kingdome dureing the reigne of his royall father and grandfather" and, that while the government of the church would be secured "in such a frame as shall be most agreeable to the Word of God, most suteable to monarchicall government and most complying with the publict peace and quyet of the kingdome",[20] kirk sessions, presbyteries and synods should continue in the meantime. Despite this promise many synods found their existence threatened owing to their hostility to the act. On 4 April 1661 the synod of Glasgow and Ayr unanimously agreed on a declaration denouncing "prelatical episcopacy"[21] and upholding presbyterian government, but when the ministers attempted to reconvene in May they were forbidden to do so by a proclamation at Glasgow cross. The synod of Fife had already suffered this fate in April when, after several declarations including one against prelacy, their deliberations were interrupted by the Earl of Rothes who commanded them to be silent and depart. Similar action was taken against the synod of Dumfries which had threatened all ministers who complied with prelacy with deposition, and the synod of Galloway who protested against the violation of their liberties. The expressed opinion in these synods was fairly unanimous against any restoration of episcopacy but other synods were more evenly divided in their views, whereas others were apparently prepared to acquiesce in change. Of those who were prepared to accept the royal will, most lay north of the Tay but even in these unanimity was only achieved by the expulsion of opponents, albeit a handful. Elsewhere depositions made little difference to the final outcome of the synod's deliberations, for while the synod of Lothian acquiesced in a demand that certain Protesters should be excluded, their removal was insufficient to secure the passage of overtures in favour of prelacy and this synod was also dissolved.

In all this the king's determination to implement an episcopal solution can be clearly seen. During May and June discussions to this end took place in London, a leading part in these being taken by James Sharp who had again journeyed south in early May. His conduct there has again been the subject of dispute, but it seems unlikely that he was directly instrumental in sacrificing presbyterianism to episcopacy but rather acquiesced in a decision made as much for political as ecclesiastical reasons. To this end the decisions ultimately reached depended not so much on the wishes of churchmen, but rather on the expedients of politicians. Amongst these, presbyterianism still had its champions as late as July 1661 but, whereas at a meeting of the Scots council in London the Earl of Crawford still argued strongly for such a settlement, its other friends such as Lauderdale, Hamilton and Sir Robert Moray were much more cautious and would only advocate further consultation with Scottish churchmen. Clarendon's taunt, "God preserve me from living in a country where the church is independent from the state and may subsist by their own acts: for there all churchmen may be kings",[22] hit at the root of their dilemma. Faced with the insolubility of this problem the waverers eventually settled in favour of the royal autocracy which others such as Middleton, Glencairn and Rothes urged upon the king at this juncture. Such advice accorded with Charles' own desires and faced with positive advice on one side and irresolution on the other, the king decided to implement an episcopal settlement. Sharp may have anticipated this verdict, which in all probability accorded with his own wishes. His views certainly were in accordance with those of Middleton's by 21 May 1661 when he expressed the hope that "all opposing designs are dashed and a foundation laid for a superstructure, which will render your name precious to the succeeding generations".[23] If he was not the villain of the piece Sharp certainly exhibited a pliancy which was tantamount to desertion of the Resolutioner cause which he purported to serve, and in this respect he undoubtedly deserved the rebukes that he attracted from his fellow Resolutioners.

With the die cast, Lauderdale was ordered on 14 August to write to the council in Scotland expressing the king's intention "to interpose our royall authority for restoring of that church to its right government by bishops".[24] The council met on 5 September and, after first refusing to accept the suggestion of Tweeddale and Kincardine that the king should be asked first to refer the matter to synods, the royal will was proclaimed at the cross of Edinburgh on the following day. The proclamation announced the abolition of presbytery because of "the unsuteablnes thereof to his Majestie's monarchical estate",[25] restored government of the church by bishops and ordered all non-conformists to be committed to prison. Coercion of the recalcitrant was already evident in a solution clearly imposed by royal fiat.

The extent to which this unilateral edict reflected national opinion has often been debated, but the evidence can leave little doubt that the wishes of the vast majority of the Scottish people were overridden in the interests of royal autocracy. If the abandonment of the covenants could be more readily justified, their appeal to a considerable section of the Scottish people was still undiminished. Indeed as the instructions to Sharp clearly indicated, the Resolutioners had high hopes in the months which preceded the actual restoration of the king that the covenants would be implemented. But such support was mainly from the ministers and from the lower echelons of society. Amongst the nobility and the more influential classes of society the covenant had lacked coherent support since the excesses of the late 1640s, and any appeal which it still possessed in 1659 was quickly dispelled as it became apparent that its aims could not be secured by negotiation. The loss of this category of support made Resolutioners and Protesters alike despair of achieving their ends as hostility to the covenant became more manifest. On the other hand, it would be unwise to accept the sentiment expressed in the following verse as typical:

> From covenants with uplifted hands
> From remonstrators with associate bands,
> From such committees as governed the nation,
> From church commissioners and their protestation,
> > Good Lord, deliver us.[26]

This was the sentiment of an articulate but small section of Scottish society, and even here the venom of the attack is directed not so much at the covenants as such but at the Remonstrants or Protesters who had attempted to implement the terms of the Solemn League and Covenant by force. This aspect of the earlier covenanting movement had certainly been rejected by all but a few before 1659, but, as long as attainment of the covenant by negotiation appeared to be possible, it still attracted considerable support. Only when the cause of English presbyterianism was seen to be irrevocably lost did this attitude change. Enforcement of the covenant by unilateral action was certainly unacceptable to the great majority of its former supporters who were prepared thereafter to settle for a presbyterian settlement in purely Scottish terms. That this was the overwhelming desire of the Scottish people, before the royal proclamation of 6 September 1661, would seem to be unquestionable. The instructions to Sharp and the dismay and opposition evinced by the largest and most influential of the presbyterian synods to the king's proposals all point in this direction. Up to this point many of the nobles and other landowners, including Lauderdale, still favoured presbyterianism as a system of church government. Among the ministers themselves some may have genuinely favoured episcopacy, others like Sharp may have been prepared to move towards it as the final solution veered in favour of bishops, but a majority clearly favoured the *status quo*. But the royal pronouncement transformed the situation. The peer who declared, "I judge myself bound in conscience to defend episcopacy with my life and fortune so long as his majesty and the laws are for it" expressed an attitude common to landowners as a whole.[27] Autocracy was to be upheld, episcopacy was to replace presbyterianism for no better reason than this was the royal will. On such grounds Lauderdale abandoned his attempt to find a compromise, which would have allowed monarchy and presbytery to co-exist, and many others followed in his footsteps. Ministers who would have preferred a presbyterian solution, but equally believed in royal authority, were similarly converted, and all the more easily so if prospects of advancement within the framework of the new establishment seemed likely. Even amongst the people at large the edict effected a transformation of opinion as support for the established church was to many Scots a much more important tenet than support for either episcopacy or presbyterianism. Such an attitude was all the more easily encompassed in so far as the services of the church remained virtually unaltered in consequence of the move from one form of organization to another. Such considerations, rather than any genuine change of heart, produced a situation in which the newly-established episcopal church could claim with some confidence to represent a majority of the people, but ranged against this amorphous institution was a committed body of presbyterian dissent.

The implementation of the royal edict may have strengthened this opposition and the nomination of James Sharp to the vacant archbishopric of St Andrews on 14 November 1661 certainly strengthened the suspicions of those who had come to suspect his double-dealing. Other nominations went the way of men who had already revealed a facility to change allegiances to suit their personal convenience. Foremost amongst these was James Hamilton, who became a rigid Covenanter following his deposition in 1639 and now became Bishop of Galloway, and Robert Leighton, who had made a pretence of accepting the covenant in 1643. In accepting the see of Dunblane Leighton made no secret of his motives at that time, and not for the first or last time in his life was revealed as a man to whom solemn promises meant little. This was more than adequately revealed when Sharp, Hamilton, Leighton and Andrew Fairfoul, who had been nominated to the archbishopric of Glasgow, were summoned to London to receive regular consecration at the hands of the English bishops. Before this could be effected it was deemed that Sharp and Leighton, who had entered the ministry after the abolition of episcopacy in Scotland, should also be episcopally ordained. Sharp, to his credit, at first refused claiming equal validity for his presbyterian orders, but received no support on this from Leighton, who was again revealed as a man of little principle. But his view prevailed and all four were consecrated in Westminster Abbey on 15 December 1661. On their return to Scotland in April of the following year they gradually proceeded to consecrate nominees to the other vacant bishoprics and by mid-summer the hierarchy was complete. Of these only one, Thomas Sydserf, who became Bishop of Orkney, had held office as Bishop of Galloway before the Glasgow assembly of 1638. Of the others some such as Bishop Mitchell of Aberdeen and Bishop Wishart of Edinburgh had suffered deposition rather than renounce episcopacy, but others such as Bishop Mackenzie of Moray had been staunch Resolutioners and Covenanters. When parliament met on 8 May 1662 nine bishops were able to answer the invitation to take their places and assist in the completion of the church settlement.

In this parliament, which sat until 9 September, acts were formally passed restoring episcopal government, declaring the covenants unlawful and equally significantly declaring conventicles illegal. Opposition to the Restoration settlement had already become sufficiently overt to warrant the forbidding of "all private meitings or conventicles in houses which under the pretence of, or for, religious exercises, may tend to the prejudice of the publict worship of God in the Churches, or to the alienating the people from their lawful pastors, and that duetie and obedience they ow to Church and State".[28] The basis of this opposition was not hard to seek. The "act for the

Restitution and Re-establishment of the Ancient Government of the church by Archbishops and Bishops" had rescinded all acts, and in particular that of 1592 by which "the sole and only power and jurisdiction" within the church "doth stand in the generall, provinciall and presbyteriall assemblies and Kirk sessions".[29] If in the event synods, presbyteries and kirk sessions were to be allowed to meet, they were only to be allowed to do so with episcopal authorization. No conscientious presbyterian could possibly have accepted, even as a compromise, a system which removed the supreme court of the church and took from two of its remaining courts—the synod and the presbytery—their distinctive hall-mark of elected moderators. No matter how amenable bishops might be in their synods or the constant moderators in presbyteries, their very existence threatened the entire basis of conciliar government within the church. With these bishops also appointed by the state, the Erastian character of the establishment made it equally inevitable that the system would be unacceptable to many. The vestiges of power left to synods and presbyteries in no way compensated for these fundamental changes. If in matters of worship there was less to cavil at, in so far as there was no return to the Five articles or a compulsory prayer book, the use of such a book was not unknown and if the re-introduction of the doxology, the Lord's Prayer and Apostles Creed were pleasing to some, others were to regard them as "rotten wheel-barrows to carry souls to hell".[30] How far these objections would have expressed themselves in open schism is open to doubt, although there is every indication from 2 January 1662 when the council received a letter from the king forbidding all ecclesiastical meetings in synods, presbyteries and sessions, until authorized by the prelates, that opposition would not remain dormant. A further act of 11 June declaring all parishes to be vacant whose ministers had been appointed since 1649, unless they applied for and received presentations from the former patrons as well as collation from their diocesan bishop before 20 September 1662, made active opposition inevitable.

Chapter Three

THE CHURCH DIVIDED

THE INTENT BEHIND the Act for Presentation and Collation of June 1662 is not entirely clear. The validity of presbyterian orders was not in question but, in so far as it provided an opportunity for the immediate revival of patronage in parishes in which patrons' rights had been abrogated at the last vacancy, it may have been intended as a practical demonstration that such rights would be safeguarded in the future. But in all likelihood the real intention was to oust a few prominent Protesters from their charges. In the event, however, opposition was not to be confined, either to a few, or to Protesters. Instead government policy had the effect of thrusting together the two wings of the Protesting party (Erastian and anti-Erastian) whereas skilful diplomacy might have separated those who were willing to accept the king's authority from those who were not. At the same time it allied to these the anti-Erastian wing of the Resolutioners.

The extent of initial opposition to the edict can best be judged by examining attendances at diocesan meetings called by the council on 10 September 1662 for early October of that year. But even before these meetings revealed the extent of the defections from the church, it had become apparent that in the dioceses of Glasgow and Galloway few would seek collation or attend the diocesan meetings. In the hope of securing obedience Middleton accompanied by members of the council decided to perambulate the south-west, and, on the assurance of Archbishop Fairfoul that not ten in his diocese would ultimately stand out, the council agreed on 1 October to extend the period for complying with the act until 1 November. Neither the progress, which lasted until 31 October, nor the extension of the date led to any significant change of attitude, and in the meantime the diocesan meetings had confirmed that conformity in the west was at a premium. In the diocese of Glasgow only 27 ministers obeyed the bishop's summons. If in the east attendance was somewhat better, 58 ministers attending a meeting in the diocese of Edinburgh, there were still considerable defections. This was equally true of the diocesan meeting of St Andrews from which many ministers from Fife absented themselves. Elsewhere attendances were much fuller and the pattern of deprivations which was to emerge in 1663 was already beginning to take shape. One further respite was, however, offered, the date for compliance being finally set at 1 February 1663. But even fewer took advantage of this further extension, and, long before this time-limit had expired, ministers had begun to withdraw from their parish churches.

The council on its part had anticipated the successive deadlines and many recalcitrant ministers who had refused to sign the oath of allegiance unless they were allowed specifically to exclude the king's spiritual authority were called before parliament. All but one, William Adair minister of Ayr, expressed their scruples in a written submission, and for their pains were imprisoned and only released under sentence of deposition and expulsion from their parishes. Others expelled before the end of 1662 included three ministers of Edinburgh: Donald Cargill minister of the Barony church of Glasgow, John Blackadder, minister of Troqueer, and John Welsh, minister of Irongray. These three were to remain bitter opponents of the Restoration settlement and became active participants in the conventicling movement. John Brown, minister of Wamphray, arrested and imprisoned in November 1662, also became an active protagonist after his punishment and release, but in company with his fellow exile Robert MacWard, former collegiate minister of the Outer High church of Glasgow, he was to wage his opposition with his pen. If Welsh, and to a lesser extent Blackadder, were to exhibit some sense of moderation in the conflict ahead, Brown and MacWard were destined to exercise through their writings an uncompromising battle against the state which Cargill and later adherents such as Cameron and Renwick were left to translate into practical terms. Action against such recalcitrants was, until the end of 1662, reserved for Protesters and others who were considered most dangerous to the stability of the church, but even with this reservation some 200 depositions had been effected before the period of grace finally expired on 1 February 1663. Thereafter the deposition of the less important dissidents commenced. In March, thirteen ministers in the presbytery of Kirkcudbright, six in Stranraer, six in Wigtown and two in Dumfries were deprived and, at the same time, fourteen ministers in the synods of Perth, Fife and Stirling were removed from office. Gradually all ministers who had failed to seek presentation and collation were deposed, as were several others who, having been regularly presented by a patron before 1649, were legally outwith requirements of the act, but were nevertheless deposed for contumacy. Of these, some like William Guthrie of Fenwick, a prominent Protester who managed to avoid deposition until October 1665 both on this score and through the protection of his patron the Earl of Eglinton, were able to escape judgment for some considerable time, but others were not so fortunate. That few, if any, ultimately escaped in the diocese of Glasgow was almost certainly due to the vigilance of Alexander Burnet, who succeeded Fairfoul in the archbishopric after the latter's death on 2 November 1663. Other bishops, including Sharp, were more compromising in their attitude and this undoubtedly helped to minimize the total number of deprivations at this time.

The final total of depositions remains a matter of dispute. The figure has on occasions been artificially inflated by the inclusion of ministers deprived by the Resolutioners at the period of the Restoration. But, technically, as this was presbyterian replacing fellow presbyterian, the deposed Protesters may be excluded from the final tally of those who refused to conform to episcopacy. Even then difficulties remain, for, whereas the number of actual deprivations for non-conformity can be fairly accurately assessed, the fact that these depositions range over a period of five or six years inevitably means that a considerable number escaped deprivation by death. It is equally likely that any successor appointed after the royal proclamation of 6 September 1661 would support episcopacy rather than the proscribed establishment and this factor too helps to produce an anti-presbyterian weighting. In this respect it would be unwise to take figures based upon the state of affairs at 1 February

1663 as representing the state of ecclesiastical opinion some eighteen months before and equally unrealistic to equate the number of deprivations as representing the total number of ministers opposed to the settlement enforced in 1661. The exact number of ministers openly opposed to episcopacy at that point in time cannot be accurately assessed, but it clearly must have been in excess of 300. To this extent at least, one third of the established ministry of approximately 952 had been prepared to sacrifice their calling and their livelihood for presbyterian principles, and just under one third remained to carry this into effect. The extent to which the remaining two thirds were at this juncture equally committed to the concept of episcopacy is equally difficult to determine. A quarter of a century later over half the ministers of the established episcopal church were to be deprived for non-conformity following the Revolution of 1688. But comparisons between the situation then and that in 1663 are not entirely valid. Many more concessions were to be allowed to presbyterian prejudice in the early 1660s than presbyterians were prepared to allow supporters of episcopacy in 1688–9. In the post-Restoration era only a handful of the nobility and landowners continued to support presbyterianism, whereas influential support and sympathy for a non-conformist episcopal church was forthcoming from many influential quarters after the Revolution. The two situations are not comparable and in this respect the presbyterian stand in 1662–3 was all the more remarkable. The extent of lay support was even more exceptional, for, if presbyterianism was a cause deserted by all but a handful of influential supporters, the tenant farmers and lower classes of society, many of whom had much to lose in defying not only the established church but also the established order of society, demonstrated in certain areas at least an overwhelming support for presbyterianism.

Regional statistics must be interpreted as warily as those at a national level but, to the extent that certain districts show a strong proclivity one way or another, their message is fairly clear. In this respect the area south of the Forth-Clyde line possessed as many ministers against the established church as for it. In the synod of Galloway 34 ministers from 37 parishes were deprived before 1666, and, if no other synod could quite match these figures, the synod of Glasgow and Ayr lost over two thirds of its ministers and the synod of Dumfries just over half. In the east deprivations were fewer, but at least one third of the clergy in the synod of Lothian and Tweeddale and that of Merse and Teviotdale were ousted. If the numbers of ministers deprived in these areas were considerably less than in the west, the support accorded to Conventiclers in the east during the 1670s would seem to suggest that the action of many ministers in remaining within the establishment did not by any means have the wholehearted support of their parishioners. But these sentiments were not shared north of the Tay. The number of deprivations north of that river was on a relatively small scale with six each in the synods of Aberdeen and Angus and the Mearns. Other synods, including Ross, could only muster nine depositions between them. Presbyterianism had clearly few adherents amongst the ministers in this particular region. The structure of society in many of these areas, every bit as much as innate ecclesiastical conservatism, may have contributed to this state of affairs. But be this as it may, what was certain was that in the final outcome ecclesiastical controversy would be decided, as it had been in the past, without reference to the wishes of the north. This had been the case since the Reformation onwards and in this respect the attitude of the central belt was critical to the final outcome. In terms of actual deprivations the support for presbyterianism in this region seemed slight as the majority of ministers in this area conformed. Only about one minister in three chose to be deposed, nineteen suffering this fate in the synod of Fife, eleven in the synod of Perth and Stirling and in the far west, fourteen in the synod of Argyll. But in Fife, at least, later conventicling activity appears to suggest that ministerial conformity cannot always be taken as a reliable guide to popular wishes.

When these regional figures are re-aggregated at a national level, several significant patterns appear. If the area north of the Tay appears fairly solidly episcopal with only isolated pockets of dissent, the area south of that line presents a picture in which the ministry was almost evenly divided. As far as the laity is concerned the picture is more difficult to determine, but, in so far as presbyterian solidarity appears to have been greater in the parishes of the deprived ministers than episcopal solidarity in the conformist parishes, the presbyterians may well have been in the majority south of the Tay. In practical terms this may be accounted a more important advantage than a numerical majority derived from remote areas such as Orkney, Caithness and the Isles. The battle ahead was not to be fought on the strength of percentages and majorities, but in terms of commitment. This at least the presbyterians had in plenty, while those ranged against them appeared to represent an unstable coalition of convinced episcopal supporters, those committed to the establishment principle and the apathetic. If commitment had played any part in deciding the issue between presbyterianism and episcopacy this factor, as at the Reformation, might have been deemed as important as a simple majority verdict. But in the event the only consideration was government convenience and this dictated that presbyterian dissent should be curbed as a threat to royal autocracy.

This campaign had commenced long before the final failure of the attempts to maintain the unity of the church. In addition to the eviction and banishment of ministers from 1660 onwards, the fining of dissidents became standard practice. An Act of Indemnity in 1662 excluded from its general provisions a list of some 700 persons who were only to be allowed oblivion for their previous actions if they paid fines ranging from £200 to £18,000 Scots. Some of the fines were destined for Middleton's own pocket, and the precedent thus set was to characterize the collection of many of the later fines levied for religious dissent. Yet another exception to the Act of Indemnity was, however, to lead to Middleton's dismissal as commissioner. In an effort to consolidate his own position, Middleton suggested to the king that twelve persons selected by parliament should be excluded from public office as unreliable agents of the crown. Among the twelve ultimately selected were Sir Robert Moray and Lauderdale, but in this attempt Middleton had over-reached himself. Lauderdale was not only able to prevail upon the king to suspend the payment of fines, and recall the attempted exclusion bill, but also to secure the dismissal of the commissioner in March 1663.

The new commissioner, the Earl of Rothes, fell heir to all the problems which Middleton's administration had created. The two most pressing problems were the replacement of almost one third of the church's ministry, and that of muzzling the deposed ministers. Neither of these tasks was to prove easy. In the less disaffected areas patrons were only too willing to nominate replacements, but in the south-west patrons, who were sympathetic to the deprived preachers, showed a singular reluctance to present and the onus of finding suitable ministers devolved on the crown. The quality of these "king's curates" who were intruded into parishes has been the subject of dispute, but the general consensus of opinion has been unfavourable. Setting aside the most scurrilous of the comments, they could nevertheless be described by the contemporary historian Gilbert Burnet as "the worst preachers" he had ever heard: "they were ignorant to a reproach and many of them were openly vicious. They were a disgrace to orders, and the sacred functions: and were indeed the dregs and refuse of the northern parts".[1] Sir Robert Moray, a moderate presbyterian and advocate of toleration, concurred in this verdict and observed that it was impossible to support such ignorant and scandalous men, "unless the greatest part of them could be turned out".[2] These judgments have been tempered by the observation that Burnet was no less critical of presbyterian ministers who possessed in his estimate "a very scanty measure of learning".[3] It is equally true that the curates every bit as much as their opponents were university educated, but this may be as much a stricture on university education at this time as a defence of their educational attainments. What is undeniable is that for one reason or another the curates had failed to obtain a church living until this opportunity arose. Despite presbyterian gibes about their youth, most of the curates were mature unbeneficed ministers. In the parlance of a later age, they were "stickit ministers" who had been engaged as tutors and in other non-ministerial functions until this period. In this respect, if in no other, they may have lacked the qualities which were required in a parish minister at this time. In most cases it mattered little. As creatures of the state willing to lend their assistance to Erastian synods and presbyteries, they were totally unaccept-

able to all but a few. Many of the curates found induction into their new charge could only be secured by military
intervention. At Irongray the new incumbent who was to
replace Welsh fled before a hail of stones from the women of the
parish, and a similar riot characterized an attempted induction
at Kirkcudbright in early 1663. Such violence inevitably
brought retaliation, and a commission appointed by the council
in May to bring the malefactors to justice was one of the first
of many which were to exact for themselves free quarters and
provisions, and thus establish a standard pattern for future
military action. The trial of the offenders was equally indicative of future action. The principals were remitted to Edinburgh for trial, after which one was banished and two heavily
fined. Five women from Kirkcudbright who stood trial with
them were returned to their native burgh to stand for two days
at the cross of Kirkcudbright with a placard announcing their
crime. Resistance did not characterize the filling of every
vacancy, nor indeed was every vacancy immediately filled, but
slowly but surely, by one means or another, the pulpits of the
deprived ministers were gradually bestowed upon others. To
place these ministers was one thing, to provide them with a
congregation was quite another.

In many parishes throughout the south-west the congregations had followed the example of their ministers and deserted
their parish churches. Thereafter they heard the gospel
preached in houses and barns or in the fields. Such meetings,
known as conventicles and their adherents as Conventiclers,
grew in extent and in the number of their adherents as more
and more ministers were deposed during 1661. Inhibitions,
directed against individual ministers ordering them to withdraw from the bounds of their former parishes or even from
the realm, had sought to curb the problem in its early stages,
but by 1662 a general act against conventicles had been deemed
necessary. Such meetings inevitably constituted a direct
challenge to the whole fabric of the ecclesiastical settlement and
as this became increasingly evident, further action against
deposed ministers became necessary. With the settling of the
"king's curates", who often found themselves preaching to
diminutive congregations, the associated problem of non-church

going also came to the fore. By mid-1663 action was required on two fronts and it was to these problems that the policies of the new commissioner were to be initially directed.

The arrival of Rothes in Edinburgh on 15 June 1663 saw the initiation of these policies. Allies in this cause were enlisted by the admission of the archbishops of St Andrews and Glasgow to the council, and three days later parliament met and subsequently proceeded to enact legislation designed to produce religious conformity. On 10 July an act was passed ratifying the ecclesiastical statutes of the preceding session and it was further enacted that "all and every . . . person or persons who shall heirafter ordinarly and wilfully withdraw and absent themselffs from the ordinary meitings of divine worship in their oune paroche church on the lord's day (witherupon the accompt of poperie or other disaffection to the present government of the church)" should be fined.[4] With this enactment —"the bishops' Drag Net"—and the ratification of the act against Conventiclers, the necessary statutory authority to proceed against conventiclers, on either or both counts, had been obtained. But not all deprived ministers were overt conventiclers, and, in order to ensure total compliance with these edicts, council enacted on 13 August 1663 that all recalcitrant ministers should either conform within twenty days or remove with their households twenty miles from their churches, six miles from a cathedral city and three miles outside a royal burgh. This legislation had little immediate effect and conventicling actually appears to have increased as the south-west became a place of refuge for several Irish presbyterian ministers who had been evicted from that country on the restoration of episcopacy there.

Military intervention was increasingly regarded as the only possible solution to a problem which was rapidly getting out of hand. In September 1663 Sir James Turner was ordered to Kirkcudbright after a local contingent of foot guards had failed to prevent a young non-conformist minister, Alexander Robertson, from preaching in the vacant church of Anwoth. Armed forays of this nature tended to encourage the assumption that ultimate success would follow if activity in this direction was increased. The new Archbishop of Glasgow,

Alexander Burnet, emerged as a strong advocate of such a policy and the military repression which characterizes the years 1664–5 owes much to his personal inspiration. Sharp, on the other hand, was always more cautious in this respect, preferring more subtle, and none the less effective, means of encouraging religious conformity. To this end, Sharp advocated the re-establishment of the Court of High Commission which he secured by a warrant of 16 January 1664. Every ecclesiastical offence was to come under the survey of a tribunal which was to last until November of that year and was empowered to fine or imprison without indictments, defences or evidence led. The court dealt with a great variety of offences, including several of alleged disrespect to intruded curates and withdrawal from services of the established church. The oath of allegiance enacted in 1663, which entailed recognition of the king's spiritual authority, became the touchstone in many of these cases. Offers to take the oath in a modified form were unacceptable and James Hamilton, the laird of Aitkenhead near Cathcart, was not alone in being financially ruined by his stand on this score. Punitive measures on this scale could deal with individual cases of disobedience: it effectively removed a few more dissident ministers such as William Guthrie of Fenwick, but it could not solve the more widespread problem of conventicling and non-church going in dioceses such as Glasgow and Galloway.

In these areas conventicling was not only increasing as many of the deprived ministers such as Welsh and Blackadder became bolder and increasingly far-ranging in their activities. Banished from their own parishes they travelled far and wide inciting others to follow their example and drawing ever increasing numbers from their parish churches. Their names and others, such as that of Alexander Peden former minister of Glenluce, soon became almost a legend in their own lifetime. By the close of 1665, they and other associated ministers had become wanted men. In fear of arrest they armed themselves and were often protected by armed followers. Conventicles imperceptibly changed their character from that of groups of worshippers gathered for prayer to armed convocations for whom worship was still the prime object of their meeting but who would

certainly retaliate if attacked and might, under certain circumstances, spontaneously take to arms. Faced with this realization,
Burnet's insistence on greater military intervention became
increasingly attractive to Rothes and the council in whose
deliberations the two archbishops were playing an ever important part. Of the two, Sharp may have been the more
ambitious, although his endeavours to secure the chancellor-
ship for himself following the death of the Earl of Glencairn
on 30 May 1664 proved to be fruitless; but Burnet largely
dictated policy. His influence in this direction increased as his
arguments in favour of direct military action became apparently
unanswerable after the outbreak of the Dutch war in 1665.
Many of the banished ministers had found sanctuary in Holland,
and the bond of sympathy between the Dutch and the Conventiclers was sufficiently strong to lead many to believe that an
insurrection on their behalf was not out of the question.
Burnet playing on these fears and others, including that of a
conspiracy between the Conventiclers and Ulster presbyterians,
undoubtedly used the situation to further his own predilection
for military intervention; and to this end on 3 October 1665
secured a letter from the king to the Privy Council to apprehend
a number of prominent Protesters including Robert Mont-
gomery, brother of the Earl of Eglinton, Cunningham of
Cunninghamhead, Maxwell of Nether Pollok and Campbell of
Cessnock. At the same time permission was received to proceed
against all who refused the oath of allegiance. Statutory fines
were thereafter to be imposed in full on all who would not take
both that oath and the declaration against the covenant. Sir
James Turner was once again despatched to the south-west
with 140 horse and foot guards, to ensure conformity with this
edict. In the process the scheduled fines were far exceeded,
others suffered from the quartering of soldiers, and the general
brutality of the military operation seems beyond question
although, according to a certificate subscribed by several of
those who suffered at Turner's hands, "Sir James had used
them civilly and discreetly".[5] The operation achieved its
limited objectives, but fear of insurrection still ran high and
further repressive legislation inevitably followed. On 7 December 1665 an act of eviction ordered the few remaining

ministerial recusants to quit their manses and yet another act
against conventicles declared them to be "seminaries of separation and rebellion" and frequenters of them to be traitors to be
apprehended by "all our public ministers".[6] The deft twist
whereby religious dissenters might be dealt with as traitors was
already to the fore in this legislation in which the subtle hand
of Burnet can be readily discerned.

As the fear of insurrection grew, counter measures were
hastily discussed to increase the military forces at the government's disposal. In February 1666 Archbishop Burnet was sent
to London to obtain approval for the utilization of fines as a
means of providing for a militia, and a military build-up commenced thereafter, command of this force being assigned to
Thomas Dalyell of Binns and Sir William Drummond, both
of whom had seen considerable service abroad. In retrospect the necessity for this step may be questioned, but any
remaining doubts which the council may have entertained had
been effectively dispelled by the circulation in Scotland of a
work entitled *An Apologeticall Relation of the particular sufferings of
the faithful ministers and professours of the Church of Scotland since
1660*. Written by the exiled John Brown of Wamphray and
published abroad, the book not only dwelt on the injustices
perpetrated on the upholders of the covenant but also justified
resistance to those who persecuted their cause. This was not
only a defence of the stand already adopted, but a positive call
to action. Sharp who forwarded a copy to Lauderdale charac-
teristically labelled it "a damned book" and claimed that it
had turned the country's quarrel into a defiance of the crown.[7]
In this judgment he may have been mistaken, but there is
little doubt that writings such as this influenced a significant
number in the direction of armed intervention and gave ample
justification to the assertion that supporters of the covenant
were traitors. Its practical significance at time of publication
was, however, minimal and revolt when it came was for very
practical reasons. In this respect the contrast between the west,
on which pressure to conform had been increasingly brought
to bear, and the east, in which little attention had been
paid to deprived ministers and occasional breaches of ecclesiastical discipline, is instructive. The number of presbyterian

sympathizers in the east was certainly less than in the west, but, as was to be clearly exhibited in the 1670s, the conventicling spirit and dislike of the established church had many adherents in Fife and south-eastern Scotland. These sympathies were not entirely dormant during the early 1660s but were generally exhibited by non-attendance at church, and in this respect private covenanting leading to the growth of pietism appears to have been the hall-mark of non-conformity in this and other parts of Scotland. In the west more outward demonstrations of non-conformity were almost inevitable, but it is equally certain that if they had been more tactfully handled a mass confrontation could have been avoided. Each new act of repression was met with further embittered resistance on the part of the Conventiclers and as the military build-up continued in the course of 1666 it became increasingly apparent that a military confrontation would occur sooner or later.

In the event, the conduct of Sir James Turner was to prove decisive. Sent into Galloway with 120 foot guards in March 1666 when fear of insurrection was at its height Turner, with the aid of the commission for discipline authorized on 7 December of the previous year, had been able, from his headquarters at Dumfries, to fine and outlaw even the most influential if they refused to co-operate with the curates. The screw was turned tighter and tighter until even the Bishop and synod of Galloway was constrained in October to appeal for leniency towards the heritors. But all to no avail. Turner, who returned to Galloway with the backing of the council in November, could not be dissuaded from his course of action. Greedy for fines which often found their way into his own pocket, he proceeded to collect not only the usual fines for absence from church but also to collect the fines imposed as an exception to the Act of Indemnity. The period of grace for the suspension of these penalties obtained by Lauderdale after Middleton's disgrace had now lapsed and at Burnet's insistence these were to be paid in full by all who refused to take the oath of allegiance and renounce the covenants, and by those who agreed to take these oaths at half the agreed sum. A proclamation of 11 October 1666 which made proprietors liable for the good behaviour of all who resided on their land, magistrates liable for inhabitants of burghs and masters responsible for servants added a new dimension to Turner's authority. These powers were to be considerably extended by his own initiative and among charges later levelled against him were extorting billet money for those over and above the number of soldiers actually quartered on recalcitrants, the resurrection of charges on previous offences and fining parishioners for non-church going in parishes in which no minister was settled. These injustices proved to be the last straw and as repression escalated so too did talk of retaliation. But in the event a chance occurrence, rather than concerted action, brought events to a head on 13 November 1666.

On that day a party of three soldiers led by Corporal George Deanes, engaged in collecting fines for non-church attendance at St John's Clachan of Dalry, were in the process of impounding corn belonging to a farmer named Grier in lieu of his unpaid fine, when the defaulter himself was apprehended. By chance their threat to "strip him naked and set him on a hot grid iron because he could not pay"[8] reached the ears of John Maclellan of Barscobe and his three companions, who were themselves fugitives and happened to be breakfasting in the village tavern. Their action was as swift as it was unpremeditated. The soldiers were confronted by the irate laird who shot at Deanes and thereafter bound the corporal and his company before they made good their escape. In other circumstances the affair might have been no more than an untoward incident for which the perpetrators, and they alone, would have been brought to justice. In the inflammatory state of public opinion at this time it led instead to full-scale military insurrection.

Chapter Four

THE PENTLAND RISING

TROUBLE OF THIS nature had been long expected by the authorities who, as early as 23 September 1663, had sanctioned the raising of 20,000 militia and 2,000 horse. Their fears were by no means imaginary and projects of armed resistance had clearly been contemplated. Burnet suspected that the insurgents had been in correspondence with sympathizers in England and Ireland. The presence with the insurgents of two Irish ministers—John Cruickshank and Andrew McCormick—who are later described as "main instruments of the attempt",[1] and both of whom were killed at the battle of Rullion Green, certainly gives some substance to this belief. Nevertheless, "the scuffle at Dalry"[2] had not been a preconcerted signal for revolt, but a chance event which hurried its perpetrators into an unplanned campaign. Coercion had created a flashpoint situation in which any untoward incident could have led to a similar reaction.

The consensus of contemporary opinion on the unpremeditated nature of the rising is unanimous. On 19 December 1666 Rothes described it as the work of "damd ffuls who had antispat ther taym of raysing", and ten days later Dalyell, in a letter to Lauderdale, expressed a similar opinion when he wrote "It simes this laist [rebellion] if it had not bein mistymd had bein muth mair terible."[3] Even Burnet, with his deeply suspicious nature, was forced to admit "Many things in this rising look like design, but I should suspect no man."[4]

Although unpremeditated the action of Barscobe and his companions in deciding to fight, rather than await the inevitable reprisals, found the Conventiclers not altogether unprepared. The call that all who were ready "should come in companies to Irongray Kirk on Wednesday night [14 November], that they might enter Dumfries by daybreak" drew an immediate response,[5] but there is doubt about the number who actually assembled. For whereas all authorities are agreed that 50 horse attended the muster, estimates of the number of foot range from about 200 to "some few"; the reckoning that the total number of insurgents was "a hundreth and fiftie or therby" would seem to be a close approximation.[6]

The resolution and determination exhibited by the Conventiclers was in marked contrast to that shown on the side of the authorities. If Sir James Turner, the commander at Dumfries, was immediately desirous of revenge when confronted by the wounded Deanes, who swore that he had been shot for refusing to sign the covenant, he was singularly ill-equipped to take action. Not only was he unwell, having "let blood seven times",[7] but his cavalry and half his infantry had been withdrawn for service in the Dutch war. Of the 70 men left at his disposal only twelve or thirteen were in Dumfries and of the remainder sixteen had been seized at Balmaclellan by Conventiclers who, having been apprised of the incident at Dalry, had apprehended the soldiers who were quartering nearby. Nevertheless, Turner gave orders that his troops were to be called in by nine o'clock next morning to "ressave powder, match and ball" to march on Dalry.[8]

Before the appointed hour, however, Turner himself was a prisoner. As the insurgents' 50 horse swept into Dumfries between eight and nine o'clock that morning he was taken in his lodging by a party of four. Accounts of his capture vary. Turner himself claimed that he calmly informed his captors "I need no quarter, nor could I be a prisoner, being there was no war declared".[9] On the other hand the picture drawn by his opponents of Turner, who was taken in his "nightgown, nightcap, drawers and socks" hanging out of the window in panic shouting "Quarters, gentlemen, for Christ's sake, quarters, there shall be no resistance" may be nearer the truth.[10] Turner had certainly some cause for alarm as a move to have him shot was only dropped at the insistence of Neilson of Corsock. Instead, the insurgents contented themselves with ransacking his room and impounding papers and 6,600 or 6,700 Scots merks which they found there. They then proceeded to the town cross where, with typical covenanting incongruity, they drank the king's health as a mark of their loyalty.

C

At this stage their final purpose and subsequent course of action still remained uncertain. In addition to their declaration for the king and the covenant, the insurgents are reputed to have alleged that their only "quarrel was at the bishops newly sett up in the land".[11] This theme was to re-appear at various stages of the rising. John Welsh, the deposed minister of Irongray, who met the insurgents at Dalmellington prayed there "for the king, the restoration of the Covenant and the downfall of Prelacie", and in a petition addressed to the council on 28 November the rising was attributed to "the intolerable insolencies of the prelates and their insupportable oppressions".[12] Although the covenant was frequently referred to, and was renewed by the insurgents at Lanark, its importance appears to have been symbolic rather than practical and there is certainly no indication that the insurgents thought of themselves as leaders of a presbyterian crusade. Indeed their seizure of Turner and their subsequent march by a devious route which took them to Ayr and only then eastwards via Lanark towards Edinburgh seems to have been principally motivated by the desire to petition the king and council for redress of their grievances.

This hope was forlorn from the outset. Government action, following the report of the rising by Stephen Irvine, bailie of Dumfries, was swift. On 17 November the council resolved that "heritors of the several countyes, especially of the southerne and westerne shyres, and such others as his majesties councill shall think fitt, be presently required to sign the declaration concerning the covenant, and that such as delay or refuse, be secured and looked upon as enemies to his majesties authority and government".[13] At the same time, Thomas Dalyell of Binns was ordered to Glasgow to proceed against the insurgents. In the event he did not leave Glasgow until 23 November but thereafter the pursuit was relentless, if cautious. Dalziel had little to lose and much to gain by wearing the insurgents down as they proceeded towards the capital. In Edinburgh itself, however, the council, unaware of the insurgents' real plight was busily issuing proclamations against them on the grounds that "the insurrection at Dumfreice and the western shyres is growne into ane oppen rebellion".[14] Fencible men from various parts of Scotland were ordered to mobilize, and, on 26 November, the payment of £10 sterling was authorized for horsemen to scour the countryside for intelligence of the insurgents' movements. Edinburgh was put on a state of alert with cannons from the castle being placed at the gates of the burgh, and lances and pole-axes were ordered from elsewhere.

The fears of the council were groundless. The insurgents were few in number and lacking sufficient leadership. As they drew near to Edinburgh the army included no more than a "few above one thousand".[15] Early in the campaign accession of strength had come from volunteers from Ayrshire and Clydesdale and, as they advanced from Carsphairn to Tarbolton, their ranks were swollen to about 700. At this stage some attempt was made to organize the army by appointing officers of horse and foot. Thereafter the army was joined by "neere one hundreth ill armed foot, and some fifteene or sixteene horse" who had been recruited in Galloway by John Welsh and also by some 50 horse recruited in Cunningham.[16] By 26 November at Lanark "the rebells [according to Turner] were in their greatest strength, which I avow never to have exceeded elevan hundreth horse and foot".[17] Thereafter numbers diminished. A further expected body of support from Galloway turned out to be only a handful and, as they marched upon Edinburgh stragglers and deserters became more numerous.

The condition of the men was as wretched as the weather; rain falling incessantly for much of the campaign. Wet, half-fed and weary through long forced marches over rough terrain, it is hardly surprising that they could be described as "rather like dyeing men than soldiers going to conquer".[18] Matters were made worse by a chronic shortage of weapons. The horse were armed with swords and pistols, but only some of the foot were equipped with conventional weapons and others had to be content with scythes, pitchforks and staves. Leadership was equally at a premium. In the raid upon Dumfries the insurgents had been led by a "Captain" Andrew Gray. His identity is a mystery. He was unknown to those he commanded, among whom he had evidently arrived at the muster at Irongray carrying with him, or so it is alleged, an order from an unknown person, ordering the insurgents to obey him. He is described by one writer as "ane Edinburgh merchant" but of this there is no proof.[19] After the insurgents left Dumfries Gray led them, without apparently any clear plan of action other than escaping retribution, via the kirk of Glencairn to the Old Clachan of Dalry from which he sent the baggage and money seized at Dumfries to a safe destination. He had apparently already decided to quit the enterprise and early on 17 November, with the party then at Carsphairn, he decamped "and was never seene since by any of his owne partie".[20] He appears to have headed south and was reported later to be at Newcastle but further than this nothing more was heard of him. With the disappearance of Gray the insurgents were left virtually leaderless and, had it not been for the new heart put into them by the arrival of John Welsh at Dalmellington the enterprise might have been abandoned at that stage. The appearance, three days later, of James Wallace at Bridge of Doon gave the army a man of military experience as its commander, but he and Captain John Paton were almost alone in their qualifications. As a result the attempt to appoint officers was not altogether successful as "not about four or five that had ever been soldiers before" were included among their numbers.[21] No commander, however brilliant, could have sustained such an army. On the march towards Edinburgh "except some of the chief officers there was not a captain present with the horse save one".[22]

With the failure to raise support in Edinburgh the insurgents pinned their hopes on the council hearing and remedying their grievances. Dalyell, to whom a petition to this end was addressed on 28 November, passed on their communication to the body which, however, informed him that it was "nowayes satisfied" with it.[23] Its only concession was that if the insurgents laid down their arms they would be allowed to petition for mercy. To the end the insurgents may have hoped for some peaceful ending to their enterprise, but were practical enough to withdraw to safer surroundings than the outskirts of Edinburgh. This strategic retreat brought them to Rullion Green at the foothills of the Pentlands where their escape route to the west was finally blocked by Dalyell's forces. Despite a heroic stand the end was predictable; with about 50 of their number killed only gathering darkness prevented greater slaughter as the insurgents broke ranks and fled. Government losses were negligible, in terms of men, but loss of prestige made further retribution inevitable.

The prisoners taken at the battle and in the subsequent pursuit numbered about 80; the majority of these, many of whom were wounded, were incarcerated in the "Haddock's Hole", a part of the High Church of Edinburgh, those of higher rank in the tolbooth. The attitude of the council presided over by Archbishop Sharp was predominantly in favour of revenge. A policy of extirpation was authorized and a proclamation was issued making it treason to harbour any of the 57 alleged ringleaders. Some of those named had clearly had no part in the affair and it seems certain that a more general policy of retribution against Conventiclers was envisaged. It was, however, the prisoners who were most immediately at risk; the quarter shown on the field of battle was not to be extended to the courts of law.

As a prelude to their trial, two of the prisoners—Hugh McKail and John Neilson of Corsock—were "tortured and examined in the bootes",[24] but little fresh evidence seems to have been forthcoming. The first trial was staged on 5 December when ten insurgents were condemned to death by hanging, a sentence which was carried out two days later, their ten right hands being sent to Lanark for fixture on the Tolbooth there and their severed heads despatched to various parts of the country. Further trials and executions followed: five men, including Neilson of Corsock, were hanged on 14 December and another six, including Hugh McKail, eight days later. On this occasion, however, three of the condemned and another awaiting execution had their sentence deferred, and an order to the Edinburgh magistrates "to take doune and remove the gallowes at the mercat croce" signalled the end of these executions.[25]

In the meantime the hunt for fugitives had shifted to other parts of the country. Justiciary commissions had been appointed on 5 December to apprehend, try and judge anyone suspected of participating in the rising, and little time was lost in effecting these instructions. On 19 December four men were hanged at

Glasgow and, five days later, twelve were sentenced at Ayr. Of these, two were subsequently hanged at Dumfries and another two at Irvine. Difficulty was experienced at the latter when the official hangman refused to execute the prisoners; a problem which also arose at Ayr with the execution of the eight condemned who were to die there. This problem was only resolved by offering mercy to one of the condemned, Cornelius Anderson, if he would hang the others. These sentences brought the judicial toll to an end, however, and the total of 36 executions may not be considered excessive in relation to the number of insurgents involved. On the other hand some had only cheated the gallows by dying of their wounds, and there would have been many more executions if more of the prominent insurgents had been apprehended. On 15 August 1667, 56 of the leading figures in the rising were tried in their absence and sentenced to death, but by that time some like Colonel Wallace had found security in Holland while others had secured more temporary refuge among sympathizers in the south-west.

Of those who died on the scaffold, friend and foe alike testify to their calmness in the face of death. If to Rothes they were to be regarded not as martyrs but as "damd incorrigeable phana-ticks" and "damd fules" cursed with "unparaelleled obdurd-nes", the fear that their example may have infected others may have played no small part in bringing the executions to an end despite Rothes' assertion that he was not "wearie of causing hang such rebellious traitors".[26] Other means of ensuring conformity could, however, be pursued and while these execu-tions were proceeding Dalyell marched westwards with his troops who were to be quartered throughout the west and south. For a time Kilmarnock proved to be a suitable base for renewed military oppression in Ayrshire. The death of David Finlay of Newmills who was arbitrarily shot at Dalyell's com-mand may be untypical but repression involving extortion, pillage and cruelty were the hall-marks of this military régime. This pattern was to be repeated in Galloway where troops under Turner and Sir William Ballantine provided themselves initi-ally with free quarters at Dalry and thereafter proceeded to terrorize all who were suspected of having sympathies with the conventicling cause. In all this they were ably abetted by the council from which emanated two proclamations designed to curb dissenters. The first of these on 25 March 1667 ordered the surrender by all persons residing within the shires of Lanark, Ayr, Renfrew, Wigtown and the stewartry of Kirkcudbright of all their arms and ammunition; non-jurors and non-church-goers were also to surrender their horses, if above the value of one hundred merks Scots. A second proclamation on 13 June rendered heritors and parishioners liable for fines and compensation exigible for assaults on, or affronts to, the established clergy. These injunctions provided fresh grist to the military despoilers whose activities remained unchecked until July 1667.

The termination of these excesses was heralded by a report to Lauderdale from Sir Robert Moray who had been despatched in June to report on affairs north of the border. Moray's report was ready by 9 July and revealed the full extent of military corruption. Illegal exactions by Dalyell were now uncovered as were the spoliations of Ballantine and Turner who, despite his peculation, was "a saint to Balantine".[27] The reports by those commanders of "mad phanaticks"[28] on the point of further rebellion were clearly only false rumours designed to maintain the crisis which was proving so lucrative. An enquiry by the council in February 1668 was more than to justify these accusations and, although Turner managed to retain some of his illegal gains, he was discharged from the king's service. Ballantine was more severely punished, being for a time imprisoned, fined £200 sterling, and banished. Peculation rather than over zealousness in carrying out their duties was, however, the basis of the eventual charges against them, and their policy of repression was certainly favoured by most of the Privy Council. But it was Moray's policy of conciliation which was to find favour with Lauderdale. In August 1667 the army was disbanded except for two troops of life-guards and eight companies of foot. Despite the disapproval of Archbishop Burnet of Glasgow, who felt that if Dalyell's policy had been followed "this kingdome had by this tyme [9 August 1667] been in a very happy and quiet condition",[29] a period of conciliation was to be embarked upon. Moray's proposal that all who took a bond of peace, with the exception of a few undesirables, should receive pardon and indemnity, became official policy. A proclamation to this effect was issued 9 October 1667, with the exception from its provisions of some 40 lay and sixteen clerical insurgents, the forfeited already scheduled and molesters of settled incumbents. Subscription to the bond was to be supervised by the heritors who were to dispossess any of their tenants who should refuse to subscribe. In the event 218 came to terms, some securing their release from prison as a result.

Not all were willing to subscribe, and it has been estimated that some 300 refused indemnity for their part in the Pentland Rising. Against these the council took resolute action and an order for the apprehension of 80 of them was issued, 9 May 1668. Transportation to Barbados, Virginia or Tangier was the usual fate for those who proved too obdurate. This too was the punishment increasingly meted out to those who continued to attend field conventicles. Nevertheless such meetings continued to increase and faced with this inexorable fact the council increasingly pinned their hopes on the success of their newly-adopted policy of conciliation.

Chapter Five

CONCILIATION

WITH THE TERMINATION of the excesses which had characterized the aftermath of the Pentland Rising a new administration, which was to show a greater understanding of the
amorphous nature of the opposition than their predecessors,
came into office. Rothes was effectively muzzled by being
created chancellor, no one being appointed in his place as
Lord High Commissioner until 1669 when Lauderdale himself
came north to fill the vacancy. In practice, however, the
men who administered Scotland from 1667 were directed
by Lauderdale from London where he served as a member
of the Cabal which had replaced Clarendon in that same
year.

The principal members of the new administration were
notable for their humanity and by lack of enthusiasm for
episcopacy. Sir Robert Moray was a founder member and
first president of the Royal Society to which his colleague and
friend the Earl of Kincardine also belonged. He had refused
to concur in the restoration of episcopacy by Act of Council in
1661 and had voted against the parliamentary enactment to
the same end in 1662. Of similar mind was the Earl of Tweeddale who in 1661 had advocated delay in the re-establishment
of episcopacy. If, in the event, political expediency had
dictated that episcopacy should be accepted, all three had a
marked proclivity towards tolerating non-conformists who had
refused to accept the settlement which they themselves had
opposed.

The way of alleviating the lot of non-conformists was not an
easy one. Pressure on the dissenters had readily been relieved
by the disbandment of the army, but a lasting solution was
more elusive. Throughout 1667–8, however, two policies were
to emerge, one advocated by the administration and the other
by Robert Leighton, Bishop of Dunblane. Leighton himself is

an enigmatic figure who commenced his career as a covenanted minister at Newbattle, weathered the storm created by
the Engagement, obtained the principalship of Edinburgh
university from Cromwell in 1653 against the wishes of the
ministers of the city, and in 1661 with an appropriate show of
reluctance accepted the bishopric of Dunblane. In view of this
remarkable capacity for personal survival and self advancement it is hardly surprising that Leighton has been accused as
a trimmer—a man who could subscribe to the covenant, defer
to Cromwell and accept a bishopric without any apparent
realization of the incongruity of his position. Whether his lack
or worldliness to which many contemporaries attest can be
deemed a sufficient excuse for his apparent lack of principle
must remain doubtful. But it was certainly his failure to
appreciate the basic principles which underlay the religious
controversies of the period which led him to suggest schemes
which were wholly unacceptable to both conformists and their
opponents. A man who could affirm of church government in
the era in which he lived that it was "a thing indifferent whether
it was Independency, Presbytery or Episcopacy" had not the
measure of his task and can be justifiably described as "not
a practicable man".[1]

Leighton's scheme, which had been gestating for some years
before he openly advanced it on a visit to London in 1667, can
be depicted as one for the accommodation of non-conformists.
The church was to be administered by diocesan synods presided over by bishops who were not to be allowed a negative
vote. Ministers at first attendance were to be permitted to protest that they accepted bishops only for the sake of peace, and
candidates for ordination that they regarded the bishop as
chief of the presbyters. To complete the whole, a provincial
synod was to be held every three years with power to examine
and censure bishops. Leighton's sincerity in proposing the
scheme is open to question. It was later alleged by one of his
own supporters of the scheme that the bishop "thought it
would be easy afterwards to recover what seemed necessary to
be yielded at present".[2] The same ambivalence had been earlier
demonstrated when on his consecration as Bishop of Dunblane
in 1661 he had agreed to re-ordination, thus denying the

validity of his earlier presbyterian ordination. He therefore seemingly accepted the tenet that there could be no valid ministry without bishops and yet in practice, with one solitary exception, he did not re-ordain his conforming clergy. However, in this respect, time was on Leighton's side and he may have hoped that accommodation would be an equally temporary expedient which would preserve the unity of the church.

If these were Leighton's hopes they were both optimistic and unrealistic. On one side his fellow bishops viewed with alarm his method of conducting his own diocesan synod in which he asserted members should have free voting rights. On the other side, Tweeddale, Kincardine and Lauderdale with their non-conformist sympathies and insight saw that compromise based upon expediency was not likely to appeal to more than a handful of religious recalcitrants. Instead they favoured a policy of toleration to which Leighton was equally opposed. In this at least his views were consistent with those of the other bishops. Between 1667 and 1669 as the merits of the various schemes and compromises were debated their opposition to toleration was one of the few constants. The most intractable of these opponents was Archbishop Burnet who averred that "the gospel was banished out of his diocey that day the army was disbanded".[3] In 1667 he attempted to have an official plea from the bishops, who had been called to a meeting to discuss the state of the church, brought to the king's attention. In this he was thwarted by Archbishop Sharp who although favouring continued repression exhibited more political acumen in his dealings with Lauderdale behind whose back Burnet was proposing to go. A similar move attempted at a synod held by Burnet at Peebles in October 1668 led to a petition attributing the grievances in the church to "not putting the laws in wigorous executione agains disorderly persons".[4] This was also suppressed before reaching the king whom Burnet misguidedly thought would favour his policies rather than those of the administration. In fact, however, the hysteria of the opponents of conciliation, aided by the good sense of the non-conformists, strengthened the determination of the administration to solve the problem by a policy of conciliation.

This resolution which had led to negotiations between Tweeddale and Kincardine and two leading Resolutioners Robert Douglas and George Hutcheson was temporarily shattered by the attempted assassination on 11 July 1668 of Archbishop Sharp by James Mitchell—an unbeneficed minister who became convinced that the removal of the archbishop would ease the problems facing the church. As the wave of persecution which followed this attempt died down it became clear that field conventicles were as numerous as ever while the popularity of house conventicles was steadily on the increase. Such meetings, however, presented a possible solution to the problem, for, whereas field conventicles represented an outright challenge to the authority of the established church, the ministers who conducted the indoor meetings generally avoided a head-on clash with the establishment by holding their meetings at times other than those of their rivals. A conciliatory formula authorizing worship along these lines, it was felt, would appeal to such ministers and at the same time meet Kincardine's stipulation that toleration must be "given and not taken".[5] Consequently on the strength of a collusive petition from Robert Douglas and some of the more moderate and conciliatory of the deprived ministers which Tweeddale took to court, the concession known as the First Indulgence was granted on 15 July 1669. Deprived ministers who had lived peaceably were to be returned to their own parishes or other vacant charges as nominated by the council. Such ministers were only to obtain their own stipends if they accepted collation from their bishop, otherwise they were only to receive the manse, glebe and a small allowance. Attendance at presbyteries and synods was to be obligatory or otherwise they were to be confined to their own parishes in which they were authorized only to marry, baptize and admit to communion their own parishioners. Any breach of these conditions or the preaching of any inflammatory sermons and the incumbent was to be deposed again.

These proffered concessions which were being implemented by 27 July brought a violent reaction from two quarters. They were attacked as an Erastian breach of covenant by the more irreconcilable of the Conventiclers who were unprepared to accept concessions of any kind from the state. On the other hand the less fanatical of the field preachers while equally disapproving of the Indulgence were anxious not to condemn it outright. Opposition from the established church was much more unanimous. In the end, however, only a few offered more than token resistance to their implementation and it was left to Archbishop Burnet to spell out their specific objections to the proposals. This he did in the Glasgow Remonstrance drawn up in September 1669 by the diocesan synod of Glasgow, apparently with Burnet's approval. In this document the complaint was made that indulged ministers who had previously been deprived were to be admitted to preach and be exempted from episcopal control. Reaction from both the Privy Council and the king was swift. The council ordered Burnet to retire to Glasgow and to remain there during the parliamentary session which was about to begin. The king in anger complained that "this damned paper shewes Bishops and Episcopall people are as bad on the chapter as the most arrant Presbyterian or Remonstrator".[6] In the ensuing parliament royal authority was asserted in no uncertain terms in an Act of Supremacy which declared that "his majestie hath the Supream Authoritie and Supremacie over all persons and in all causes ecclesiastical within this kingdom".[7] In terms of this act Burnet's culpability could not be overlooked. He was to be "laid aside as one uselesse and unprofitable person" and this was finally achieved in his enforced resignation on 24 December.[8]

Even before the departure of Burnet the implementation of the Indulgence had proceeded apace and by 3 March 1670 43 presbyterian ministers accepted its terms and were appointed to parochial cures, one of these John Baird at Paisley replacing Mathew Ramsay who had previously been appointed there but was unable to carry out his functions owing to ill-health. A problem also arose at Stranraer where a newly-instituted minister successfully defended his rights against those of the indulged minister who had his licence to preach withdrawn by the Privy Council. Nevertheless, 41 cures were satisfactorily settled with indulged ministers within this period. In seventeen instances the minister returned to his old parish, but in the majority of cases he took up a new charge.

The geographical location of these parishes is interesting, revealing a pattern of presbyterian dissent which demonstrates that Burnet could not have been alone in his worries as to the effect of the indulged ministers upon the areas to which they were allocated. As might have been expected, 24 of the ministers were to serve churches in the western counties of Ayr, Lanark, Renfrew, Wigtown and Dunbarton; seven others, however, were appointed to churches in Argyll. Of the remaining ten, four were to serve churches in Lothian, two in Roxburghshire and one each in Angus, Berwickshire, Clackmannanshire and Perthshire. No indulged ministers were appointed to parishes in Fife as Archbishop Sharp used his influence with Rothes to ensure this.

The position of the indulged ministers having been thus confirmed, further pressure was thereafter to be brought to bear upon them to accept Leighton's scheme for accommodation, the prospects for which had been enhanced by his translation to Glasgow first as commendator of the see in 1670 and later as archbishop from 1672. Moreover, whereas Leighton saw the Indulgence as an obstacle to the realization of his plans, Tweeddale felt that by separating the more moderate from the extreme presbyterians he would revive the feud between the Resolutioners and Protesters and thus render the indulged more susceptible to government control. However, although several conferences to this end took place from August 1670 and six ministers undertook a preaching tour of three months duration in which they extolled the virtues of accommodation, they achieved nothing. The six evangelists found that the peasantry were more than their equals in debates on the nature of ecclesiastical government, and any impact they may have made was soon undone by the fervency of the field preachers who followed them. At successive conferences at Paisley in December 1670 and Edinburgh in January 1671 even Leighton had to admit that his efforts to persuade the non-conformists into accepting his scheme were in vain. For their part his opponents would not recognize bishops as constant moderators, as the concept was a breach of ministerial parity, and also refused to attend courts thus constituted because of their Erastian nature. Tweeddale's threats that their licences would be withdrawn swayed not a single minister and far from producing division in the ranks at this time demonstrated that presbyterian solidarity was still strong. Indeed the most remarkable feature of this period of conciliation is the way in which the indulged conferred about "accommodation" not only with the remaining Resolutioners but also with the Protesters with whom they agreed "most harmoniously" to reject the scheme.[9] On the part of the non-indulged the attitude of many was expressed by John Blackadder, the ex-minister of Troqueer, who could not himself accept the Erastian solution proffered by the Indulgence but was not prepared to break "Christian fellowship". To this end he and his fellow minister, John Welsh, refused to preach in any parish in which there was an indulged minister.

With the rejection of accommodation as a means of ending the religious disputes some hardening of attitudes can be discerned and the indulged ministers were thereafter confined to their parishes. This too was an element in one further attempt to ease the problem in the grant of a Second Indulgence on 2 September 1672. In this case two non-conformists were to be appointed to vacant charges, which were particularly numerous in the west, as well as a colleague to each existing indulged incumbent, and each of these couples should thereafter be confined to their parishes. This scheme, first suggested by Gilbert Burnet the professor of divinity at Glasgow university, became operative with the nomination of 115 non-conformists in twos and even in threes to 58 parishes. Twenty-six of these nominated had already been indulged in terms of the 1669 act, and so altogether 89 new names were added to the list of indulged ministers. These, with fifteen indulged ministers not re-nominated at this juncture but still authorized to preach under the earlier act and six others who were to be presented to parishes in Ayrshire and Renfrewshire as soon as they became vacant, provide a total of some 136 indulged ministers, or approximately half of those who had been deprived in 1663.

Nomination by the council was, however, one thing and compliance with the terms of the Indulgence was quite another. As well as being confined to their parishes, rules about baptism and marriage forbade them to conduct these ceremonies for

any but their own parishioners or for parishioners of neigh-
bouring vacant parishes. Communion was likewise restricted
and the celebration was to be held by all ministers upon the
same day. Those and other regulations were not only resented
for their terms but also because they underlined the Erastian
nature of the concessions. Equally disliked was the device of
associating two or three ministers with a single parish and in
this respect the refusal of the indulged to serve parishes in such
a manner, unless the parish had been a double charge beforehand, undermined the scheme in one of its most important
aspects, as over 50 of those so nominated apparently refused
to conform and remained as deposed ministers. Nevertheless,
about 80 parishes were served by non-conformist indulged
ministers and these were to constitute an important alternative
to the established episcopal church.

The policy of the administration had not relied solely on
conciliation, however, for coupled with each of the Indulgences were further coercive measures against ministers who
had either not been indulged or refused to accept their limit-
ations. A proclamation prohibiting conventicles was issued on
3 February 1670 and stern action was taken against those
associated with them both by fines and imprisonment. Not
only field conventicles proved troublesome, however, and a
parliamentary enactment of August 1670 specifically dealt
with the problem of house conventicles which were becoming
more and more numerous in the burghs. The death sentence
was reserved for those concerned with organizing and conducting field conventicles but the definition of what constituted
such a gathering was extended to include meetings in a house
for prayer and preaching, "wher ther be moe persons nor the
house contains so as some of them be without doors".[10] Despite
such acts conventicles continued unabated, the recalcitrant
ministers preaching whenever the opportunity arose. Such
meetings were especially numerous in Ayrshire and Galloway,
but there is equal evidence of a growth in conventicles in other
parts. In July 1672 the council felt it necessary to take action
against a fairly influential cross-section of lairds, heritors and
tenants from Fife, Angus and Perthshire who were accused of
attendance at conventicles. The Perth merchant community

was heavily involved in such activities and several of their members were also charged at this time. The extent of the problem is further revealed by a warrant to the sheriffs of Fife, Perth and Linlithgow for the apprehension of persons who had attended conventicles within their sheriffdoms. A further proclamation against conventicles on 2 April 1673, which apportions blame for the lack of success of former acts to the failure of the heritors in providing information against conventicles and lays responsibility for so doing upon them, also testifies to the increase in their extent. In short the policy of Indulgences had done little or nothing to ease the conventicling problem and may even indeed be held to have promoted it. The indulged ministers having gained certain concessions seldom acted within their terms of reference as frequent complaints to the council reveal. William Weir, indulged minister of West Calder who had preached against prelacy and was imprisoned in the tolbooth in Edinburgh and eventually deposed for his offence, was not alone in his attitude. This indeed largely explains the degree of co-operation between the indulged and their other deposed brethren which, as it resulted in many of the non-indulged refusing to hold conventicles in parishes in which the indulged were ministering, left them free to turn their considerable efforts to other parts of the country which to that time had been free of conventicles but not of conventicling sympathizers. In such a situation further repression was likely to be seen as the only answer to the problem. With the retiral of a disillusioned Leighton to England in 1674 and the restoration of Burnet to the archbishopric from which he had been forced to resign some five years earlier, that course of action became inevitable.

Chapter Six

RENEWED REPRESSION— BOTHWELL BRIDGE

THE GROWTH OF conventicling was to continue apace after Leighton's retiral, although its most spectacular growth was not in the diocese of Glasgow, in which the presence of a large number of indulged ministers mitigated against such field meetings, but rather in the diocese of St Andrews. The indulgences have sometimes been mooted as the cause of the activity in this area on the grounds that presbyterians in the east were anxious to assert pressure similar to that which had allowed their fellow presbyterians in the west to take advantage of the concessions of 1669. But a conventicle had been held at Anstruther in 1668 and despite Sharp's denunciation of this "mad conventicling humour",[1] this was followed by similar gatherings at Strathmiglo in 1669 and at Beath Hill above Dunfermline in June 1670, the preacher on both occasions being John Blackadder. Four years later he held a vast gathering at Kinkell near St Andrews, and from there moved into that town itself where he again preached. The fervour exhibited at these conventicles extended right down the east coast, and at one such communion at East Nisbet in Berwickshire in 1677 the celebration was extended over three days. In the same year immense conventicles were held at Eckford in Teviotdale and Maybole in Ayrshire. At the first several prominent deposed ministers including Blackadder and John Welsh were present and officiated at a communion service attended by over 3,000 communicants under the watchful eye of armed guards. Such precautions were becoming the norm, and the possibility of such gatherings becoming the focal point of any move from a position of defence to that of a militant attack on the establishment was ever present. At Maybole Welsh was reported to have urged such a course if the godly were further provoked, and the sale of swords at the autumn fair there provided further practical proof that Conventiclers were becoming more aggressive in their attitude.

If the field coventicles were spectacular both in the number of adherents which they attracted and in the inflammatory oratory which they encouraged, house conventicles were also potentially dangerous in so far as they were frequently urban and attracted a much more influential class of society. The number of house conventicles certainly increased after the issue of the Indulgences and by 1674 constituted a serious rival to the services of the established church in many quarters. Such meetings were fairly commonplace even in Edinburgh and were not always restricted to private houses. In May 1674 a conventicle was held in the Magdalene chapel at which several prominent citizens were present. Several of those present were later apprehended and this in turn led to a demonstration by fifteen women who accosted members of the council as they entered Parliament Close on 4 June. A petition asking that liberty be granted to ministers to provide the citizens with a presbyterian form of service was presented to the council which promptly declared that the paper was seditious and the manner of its presentation a plot. The women involved, who included Lady Mersington and Johnston of Warriston's daughter Margaret, were banished from Edinburgh on 12 November, but at the same sitting the council was constrained to request the magistrates as to what action they proposed to take against the persons "who were present at a conventicle discovered upon Sunday last in the house of James Hamilton".[2] Little effective action was taken, and on 25 February 1675 the magistrates were again taken to task "anent the conventicle latly discovered at Leith Milnes and any other conventicles kept within the said city".[3] The full extent of the problem was, however, only revealed on 11 March 1675 when the council declared "it is of verity that upon the first, second, thrid and remnant dayes of the monethes of July, August, September, October, November and December, 1674, and the monethes of January and February 1675 . . . there have bein diverse conventicles keeped within the city of Edinburgh or suburbes thereof".[4] At least seven houses were involved as meeting places and those in attendance were again merchants, craftsmen, and their wives or widows. The attitude of the magistrates towards those meetings, to say the least, appears to have been ambivalent, and the move towards their suppression appears to have been initiated by the council and the military who could expect some allowance out of fines inflicted upon Conventiclers whom they apprehended.

Elsewhere a similar problem existed. The Glasgow magistrates appear to have been as reluctant to proceed against Conventiclers, and on 12 March 1675 the council felt impelled to order four companies of foot and a troop of horse to be quartered there "for the incouragement of the magistratts of Glasgow and baylie of the regality thereof and better enabling them to doe their deuty in suppressing of conventicles".[5] In the countryside, as much as the towns, house conventicles prospered. Lord Cardross encouraged house conventicles on his Perthshire estates and several of his tenants were fined on 5 August 1675 for their attendance at no less than ten such gatherings at which Cardross' chaplain, John King, frequently preached. Elsewhere conventicles came to be held in any convenient meeting place to which access could be gained. The laird of Stevenson's granary was used on several occasions while a father and son, Robert and James Hodge, were accused of making up a house suitable for such meetings. Evidence for private conventicling is to be found throughout most parts of southern Scotland during this period, but is particularly evident in eastern Scotland. The case of the parish of Carrington which was situated only ten miles from the capital is perhaps typical of many in this area. Here the established minister admitted to the presbytery on 3 July 1675 that he did not preach on week-days because he could not get a congregation. Even on a Sunday the minister appears to have been defied by his parishioners led by John Rew, the chamberlain of the proprietor Sir Archibald Primrose, the Lord Clerk-Register, who on two successive Sundays in June 1676 held conventicles at his house at which one James Rew preached. The elders had deserted the kirk session to a man and were followed by the one resident laird, Sir John Ramsey of Whitehill, who declared on 19 November "he would not come to the kirk again till he saw better order".[6] As numbers increased house conventicles tended to overspill into field conventicles and in this respect it is noted that a conventicle on 24 August 1679 in "James Willson's barn" had also a great "multitud without doors".[7]

The combination of field and house conventicles presented a formidable array of opposition for the council, which must have been thankful that these twin pillars of presbyterian support were largely confined to the areas south of the river Tay. Nevertheless, similar meetings were not unknown north of that line. Conventicles were reported in Buchan, Aberdeen-shire, in 1674 and on 10 August 1675 the council having been informed "that of late some turbulent persons have keiped seditious meitinges and conventicles in the shyr of Elgin" felt it necessary to empower the Earl of Moray to suppress any further disorders.[8] The ministers responsible for these con-venticles both appear to have come from Ross. Thomas Hog, who had been deprived as minister of Kiltearn and Lemlair in 1662, had retired to a farmhouse of Knockoudie at Auldearn where he had continued to preach and dispense the sacraments. He had been imprisoned for a few months at Forres in 1668, but continued to preach after his release, orders for his further imprisonment in 1674 being evaded until early 1677. The deprived minister of Kincardine, Thomas Ross, was also active in Moray from 1669, when he was accused of keeping con-venticles, but was not apprehended until 1675 when he was imprisoned first at Nairn and subsequently at Tain. In Ross itself Hugh Anderson, the deposed minister of Cromarty, and John McKillican, former minister of Alness, were also active Conventiclers until the latter's arrest and imprisonment for dispensing communion in the house of the Dowager Lady Munro of Foulis at Obsdale.

As conventicles became more numerous and seemingly rivalled the established church in the number of their adherents the more moderate of the deprived ministers were busily engaged in attempting to find their own solution to the prob-lems which beset the church. Their hopes in this direction apparently lay in the belief that recognition might be extended as a temporary expedient to an organized but nevertheless dis-established presbyterian church, which in turn would demonstrate its loyalty to the crown. To this end some of the recalcitrant ministers engaged in discussions in the hope of achieving some semblance of conciliar authority over non-conformist ministers. At a meeting in Edinburgh in June 1674 regulations had been suggested for licensing students who accompanied outlawed ministers, and measures had been devised for calling ministers to congregations and establishing church courts. These overtures were referred for discussion at local level before being finally approved at a further meeting in October. These meetings, which were characterized on the whole by a desire for presbyterian co-operation, became a regular feature of the period. One such meeting, which lasted for about a week, in May 1676 contained some 50 to 60 ministers and exhibited in its proceedings a far from irresponsible attitude. If unauthorized and irregular in its claim to represent a communion of the church, its assumption of the guise of a properly constituted committee with minutes of its proceedings and Alexander Forrester, minister of St Mungo, as its clerk, demonstrated its determination to supervise regular church business in an orderly and constitutional fashion. At such meetings the majority of ministers present clearly favoured some compromise with the authorities which would have permitted an increase in the number of preachers and authorized meeting places. Such discussions inevitably raised the issue of how far the state's authority could be recognized in order to achieve concessions. The split between the indulged and non-indulged was the most obvious manifestation of two very divergent views, but even within these groupings there were varying definitions of what constituted Erastianism. In an effort to heal this breach in the ranks of non-conformity a further convention of deposed ministers was held in early 1677. The majority view was conciliatory but their expressed view that indulged and non-indulged should work harmoniously together when the occasion offered was by no means unanimous. The Erastian attitude of the indulged was declared sinful by John Blackadder but even he was more moderate in his views than others such as John Welwood and Richard Cameron who refused to recognize the convention or its recommendations. Even if unanimity had been achieved it is doubtful whether the council could have offered the non-conformists many meaningful concessions, but negotiation would have been possible. As it was the uncompromising attitude of the more radical of the field preachers led them to make even more vigorous attacks upon the authority of the state. In so doing they not only created a greater gulf than before between themselves and the moderates but also intensified the council's fear of imminent armed rebellion.

The attitude of the council since the breakdown of attempts at conciliation in 1674 had been to make regulations against conventicles more and more stringent. A special committee of the council was appointed to deal with the problem. The process of fining Conventiclers was intensified and rewards were offered for the capture of the most persistent of the field preachers. On 18 June 1674 the council issued a proclamation making masters responsible for ensuring that their servants did not attend conventicles; heritors were to be similarly liable for their tenantry, while in burghs magistrates were to be held answerable for burgesses. On 16 July about 40 ministers were outlawed and resolute attempts to apprehend them were set in motion. This necessitated raising further troops which were increased at this stage by 1,000 foot and three troops of horse. In the following year the practice of garrisoning troops in houses of conventicling sympathizers was resumed, but all to little avail. Equal lack of success attended a proclamation of 1 March 1676 which attempted to tackle the problem by enforcing church attendance. Non-church goers among the laity, protestant as well as catholic, were to be fined, while ministers and their families who did not attend public worship were to be apprehended. A census was ordered of all who had taken the oaths of allegiance and supremacy and special courts were set up to uphold the laws against conventicles in no less than twenty shires including Aberdeen, Banff, Moray and Ross.

If fining and quartering were the normal ways of proceeding against Conventiclers, they were by no means the only ones. The imprisonment of field preachers became more rigorous. The new state prison on the Bass Rock in the Firth of Forth was deemed a fitting place of incarceration for the most persistent of the field preachers of whom several, including Robert

Gillespie and Alexander Peden, were lodged there during 1673–74. As pressure increased on the Conventiclers so did the number of prisoners rapidly multiply during 1676–7. Prisoners who were prepared to give bonds of caution were, however, released from time to time. Ill health was often advanced as the reason for release, and conditions on the tiny island on which there was no fresh water certainly cannot have been conducive to the prisoners' well-being. Their plight was not entirely without remedy, however, and while no prisoner was allowed his own servant, women were appointed by the governor to attend upon the prisoners who were also "to have the liberty of the isle in the day tyme . . . provyded that but two of them at once to have that liberty".[9] In an island which is only a mile in circumference and rises 350 feet out of the sea the opportunity for exercise was perhaps limited, but it was a concession which many less fortunate prisoners held in other prisons throughout the country would certainly have welcomed. It is uncertain whether the accusation is true that Lord Advocate MacKenzie on taking office in 1677 found the jails full of prisoners whom his predecessor Sir John Nisbet "had left in chains, because he had neither been bribed to prosecute them nor bribed to release them",[10] but it is unquestionable that Conventiclers were frequently detained for long periods without trial. Eight such prisoners petitioned the council for their liberty on the grounds that they had been detained "in the tolboth of Stirling thes threttine moneths to the sad loss and utter ruine of them and there poore famellies, who are most pairt put to begine for want of us who should wine their liveing".[11] Their petition was granted on condition that they gave a bond not to attend conventicles, but this they refused to do and the council then ordered their transportation which, with the exception of one prisoner who was thought to be dying, was duly effected. In pursuing this course of action the council can be accused of a degree of vindictiveness, but it can be equally maintained that a consistent policy following the rule of law was being maintained. Liberation from prison could normally be secured by subscription of a bond promising not to attend conventicles. Finding sufficient surety against the breaking of this promise posed a problem for the very poor, but refusal to take the bond, rather than failure to find caution, appears to have lain behind most extended confinements.

Only in one case does the council appear to have acted with scant regard for normal judicial processes. This was in the rather unusual case of James Mitchell, who was apprehended on 7 February 1674 and charged with the attempted assassination of Archbishop Sharp six years earlier. Mitchell on promise of his life confessed his guilt to a committee of the council but refused to re-affirm this before the Justiciary Court because he feared that the council's sentence of forfeiture and loss of his right hand would be set aside for the death penalty. The quandary of proving the charge was not resolved, and Mitchell remained in the Edinburgh Tolbooth from which he tried to escape in December 1675. Early in the following year he was again arraigned and charged with taking part in the Pentland Rising to which he had also earlier confessed. Torture in the boots failed to extract any further confession and he remained untried for a further year in the tolbooth until his removal in January 1677 to the Bass where he was specifically exempted from the privilege granted to his fellow prisoners of exercising on the island. There he remained for another year but was returned for trial in January 1678 after the discovery of a fresh plot on Sharp's life. Mitchell was now charged under an obsolete statute which made it a capital offence to assault a privy councillor. The only proof remained his retracted confession but this was now allowed as evidence while at the same time several of the council, including Archbishop Sharp, perjured themselves by swearing that no mercy had been promised and then intimidated three of the five judges into disallowing the plea of Mitchell's counsel for the production of the register which could prove this point. A packed jury completed the task and Mitchell was sentenced to death. To his credit Lauderdale, who had concurred in this caricature of justice, wished a reprieve, but the archbishop insisted that a pardon would encourage others in similar designs, and so the duke jestingly sent Mitchell to "glorify God in the Grassmarket".[12] As a would-be assassin Mitchell should perhaps command little sympathy, but the manner of his trial and condemnation were such that he inevitably became a symbol for those who opposed the dictates of church and state.

Poems, pasquils and satires denouncing the execution of Mitchell were responsible for adding a new dimension to the conventicling struggle. Passions that were already aflame were further excited by the transmission amongst the masses of rumours and half-truths to which no ready reply could be given. If popular discontent could be fanned in this manner, the attitude of many of the field preachers themselves was to be kindled by a constant barrage of inflammatory pamphlets emanating from exiled preachers in Holland. The two most zealous of these pamphleteers were John Brown, the ousted minister of Wamphray, and Robert MacWard, formerly minister of the Outer High church of Glasgow, who became Scots minister at Rotterdam. In his *Apologetical Relation*, published in 1665, Brown had argued against hearing any ministers of the established church, whereas many to that date had been content only to absent themselves from services conducted by intruded ministers. The case for accommodation as advocated by Leighton had been attacked by MacWard in *The Case of Accommodation* and both men from the security of exile had bitterly opposed the Indulgences and all who accepted them. Their views on these reached a new level of hysteria in 1678 with the publication of MacWard's pamphlet, *The Poor Man's Cup of Cold Water ministered to the Saints and Sufferers for Christ in Scotland* and Brown's *The History of the Indulgence*. The first of these launched a bitter attack against the Act of Supremacy while the second inveighed against the "abomination of the Indulgence".[13] This bitter attack strengthened the resolution of many of the field preachers against the indulged ministers, who found increasingly that their services were competing with conventicles. As the repressive measures advocated by the council against Conventiclers as distinct from the indulged became more severe, the very repression which had united all presbyterian dissenters in 1663 became a divisive one, and the remaining Conventiclers who were now more exclusively hard-line Covenanters became bitterly divided from the indulged.

This feeling was heightened by the increased repression which followed the execution of Mitchell and characterized the years 1678–9. In August 1677 the proclamation of 1674 requiring land-owners to become surety for their tenants had been re-issued. But with the growth of conventicling in the meantime very different conditions now prevailed. The heritors of Clydesdale refused to comply with an edict which they considered impracticable, whilst those of Ayrshire took a similar stand and urged greater leniency and more general toleration of presbyterian dissenters. The council who were being constantly bombarded with rumours of incipient rebellion were in no mood for such advice. Lauderdale set about raising support among the highland clans and asked the king for further instructions. The reply was to place Scotland under martial law and to muster English and Irish troops at Newcastle and Belfast. On 26 December 1677 a commission for raising the highlanders was issued and by 24 January of the following year the host was ready under the guidance of a commission of council to advance from Stirling to Glasgow. Thereafter, the commission set about its task of enforcing agreement to the bond by fining and quartering troops upon all recalcitrants. The mere fear of such treatment had made the heritors of Fife submit but in the south-west with the exception of Dumfriesshire the full rigours of persuasion employed by the highland host had frequently to be applied. By the end of February the coercion was all but complete and the highlanders were withdrawn leaving behind impoverished, bitter land-owners whose ability and desire to honour the bonds to which they had forcibly submitted was more than doubtful. This exercise in repression may have been deemed successful by Lauderdale who was praised for his efforts by the king but several members of the nobility were already having doubts about the wisdom of a policy which achieved little beyond the impoverishment of their tenants. Complaints to the king in March 1678 achieved nothing, and with royal approval the policy of repression continued as it became clear that enforced bonds could not in themselves curtail the holding of conventicles.

In this respect the attitude of the council was hardening towards Coventiclers. In dispersing a large house conventicle held in May at Williamwood in Renfrewshire the dragoons seized about 60 prisoners who were taken to Glasgow and after

examination offered their freedom if they subscribed the bond.
The majority who refused to subscribe were taken to Edinburgh and examined before the council which ordered their
banishment to the royal plantations in the East Indies. Other
Conventiclers including the deposed minister Alexander Peden
were to be similarly punished by transportation to Virginia,
and although in this instance failure of the consignee to receive
the prisoners in London, and the subsequent refusal of the
skipper to accept them on his ship, resulted in their liberation
and stealthy return to Scotland, transportation now became a
recognized means of dealing with Coventiclers whereas previously this punishment had been used but sparingly. Even
more stringent action had followed a conventicle held at
Whitekirk in East Lothian at which armed resistance was
offered and one of the soldiers killed. Several of the Conventiclers having been apprehended were charged with being
present at the conventicle and one of them James Learmont
was eventually executed, not for the killing of the soldier, in
which he clearly had no part, but for the capital offence of
attending a field meeting. If from a purely legal point of view
the sentence was justified, its implementation is a further
indication of increasingly severe policies. Not unnaturally the
Conventiclers on their part took greater precautions. A vast
conventicle, some 14,000 strong held on Skeoch hill in Irongray parish near Dumfries, was attended by armed and
mounted gentlemen from Lanarkshire and Nithsdale. Such an
assembly quickly took on the guise of an army who were
prepared to resist any attempts at dispersal by troops, who on
their part became increasingly prone to use their arms in
scattering conventicles.

The escalation of the conflict brought a solution no nearer.
Troops were once again sent in considerable numbers and
settled as military garrisons at Lanark, Glasgow, Dumfries,
Kirkcudbright and Ayr. Instructions for the suppressing of
conventicles and the punishing of their adherents poured forth
from the council but all to little avail. Three of the most
militant of the field preachers, John Welsh, Gabriel Semple
and Samuel Arnot, were declared traitors but could not be
apprehended as the military increasingly lost touch with the

situation. Conventicles in the south-west never totally dispersed and met in predetermined places each Sunday where they were joined by other adherents. As they grew in strength it is obvious their aims began to shift as the opportunity for exerting pressure upon the king and council for the implementation of their demands became more and more feasible. What these demands were to be was never entirely certain, but it seems obvious that although the principles of the covenant were still accepted the solution to be demanded was seen within a Scottish framework. Within this context all would have agreed that a presbyterian establishment within the church was their ultimate goal, but as to the nature of that church and its relationship with the state opinion was deeply divided.

The creation of the opportunity to present their demands was manifest in the aggressiveness displayed by the Conventiclers at this juncture. Towards the end of March two or three troopers were surprised in their quarters at Lesmahagow, and, after a conventicle in the same parish, a party of dragoons, who had seized a few stragglers, were in turn attacked by the Conventiclers who secured the release of the prisoners and themselves seized seven dragoons and wounded their commander. The murder of two soldiers followed on 20 April, and, although the murderers' religious affiliations are questionable, it is clear the continuance of a large body of men in arms was conducive to such incidents.

In Ayrshire landowners who were otherwise sympathetic to the presbyterian cause sent a deputation to the council expressing their detestation of these armed Conventiclers and the outrages which were following in their wake. This move might be attributed to political prudence but their accusations against "a few unsound turbulent and hot-headed preachers, most part whereof were never ministers of the Church of Scotland" and to whom they attributed schism,[14] separation and rebellion were probably fairly representative of moderate presbyterian opinion. In Ayrshire and in Lanarkshire the situation had clearly got out of hand, but there was equal danger other areas might follow suit. Repression undoubtedly bred resistance but the council, unmindful of this maxim, pressed ahead with such policies wherever it was in its power to do so. The sheriffs-depute commissioned by the council on 27 February set about their task of holding weekly courts to extinguish dissent, and this task was nowhere more willingly undertaken than in Fife in which the depute William Carmichael of Easter Thurston showed himself to be even more zealous in the exercise of his duties than Claverhouse and Grierson of Lag in the south-western shires. His depredations, as much as the religious zeal of the oppressed Conventiclers, brought about the conspiracy to assassinate this oppressor and the archbishop of St Andrews who seemingly encouraged his actions.

This plot had been thoroughly discussed by a fairly large number of conspirators most of whom appear to have accepted the proposal without too many qualms as God's wish and in this attitude the conspirators and many other Conventiclers were to persist. In the event, however, only twelve men set out to implement their plot and only nine of these took part in the actual murder of Archbishop Sharp. The actual deed was partly fortuitous, the primary object of their wrath on 3 May was Sheriff Carmichael who, however, on being warned that something was afoot had abandoned his hunting plans and returned to Cupar. Thereafter the conspirators appear to have been rather aimless in their actions. When informed of the approach of the archbishop, who was returning from a council meeting held in Edinburgh two days previously, they were caught without any clear plan of action. The subsequent chase of the archbishop's coach, which almost escaped them, and the way in which the would-be assassins, who included two lairds—David Hackston of Rathillet and John Balfour of Kinloch—six sons of tenant farmers in Fife and a weaver, Andrew Guillan of Balmerino, revealed their identity as they brutally murdered the archbishop demonstrates a clear lack of forethought as to the execution of the actual deed.[15]

The murder of the archbishop proved to be a turning point for both parties in the conflict. The council redoubled its efforts to curb the Conventiclers and in particular mounted an intensive drive to bring the actual murderers to justice. The assassins had, however, as much by good luck as by good judgment escaped to the west where they could expect to find a greater degree of security. In this they were not entirely disappointed and immediate government action to apprehend the murderers was far from successful. Indeed only two of the murderers, Hackston of Rathillet and Andrew Guillan who were hanged in 1680 and 1683 respectively, were brought to book for their crime, and although another, James Russell in Kettle, was apprehended in Ireland in 1680 he evidently eluded his captors. Yet another William Dingwall was killed at Drumclog, but the other six appear to have escaped scot-free. The price which had to be paid by their fellow Conventiclers was however considerable. On 4 May the council issued a Hue and Cry, with the names of the assassins printed in red, offering a large reward for their seizure, attributing the murder to the Conventiclers and ordering land-owners in Fife to gather all inhabitants at four centres for examination. At the same time action against Conventiclers in terms of fining and imprisonment continued apace.

In other respects too the Conventiclers were not unaffected by the murder of the archbishop. The assassins may have justified their task as self-appointed executioners but to other Conventiclers such action was indefensible. This division was but one of many which were driving a deep wedge between moderates and extremists at this juncture. Welsh and other prominent field preachers who had organized the early stages of the move towards militant mass conventicles were rapidly becoming supplanted by even more radical ministers amongst whom the most prominent was Richard Cameron. After his return from the continent, to which he had retired after an initial disagreement over the role of the indulged early in 1677, Cameron emerged as an even more determined opponent of Erastianism. He and other like-minded ministers, such as Donald Cargill, encouraged by the pamphlets of MacWard and Brown held services in the parishes of the indulged in which they denounced the sins of indulgence. More moderate presbyterian ministers remonstrated in vain and when they finally cited him to appear before them for presbyterial discipline and instruction Cameron obeyed but refused to accept their authority.

This fanaticism was, however, more prominent among the laity than among the clergy. Among this group were to be found three of the murderers of Sharp—Balfour of Kinloch, Hackston of Rathillet and James Russell—but their undisputed leader was Robert Hamilton, younger son of Sir Thomas Hamilton of Preston and Fingalton. As commander of an ambulatory conventicle he had already contemplated open rebellion and the accession of the three assassins to this gathering appears to have finalized his decision which was taken at a conventicle at Avondale on 25 May. A deputation which included Hamilton and Hackston met with Donald Cargill and John Spreul, town clerk of Glasgow, in the burgh and approved a manifesto which was adopted at a meeting in Strathaven and published at Rutherglen on 29 May. On that day, which was a public holiday in honour of the king's birth and restoration, some 60 to 80 Conventiclers rode into Rutherglen where after a short service Hamilton read the manifesto in which "as true members of the Church of Scotland" they denounced the statutes establishing episcopacy, renouncing the covenants, ousting the ministry, setting up royal supremacy and authorizing the Indulgence.[16] They further condemned all illegal acts of the Privy Council, but decided against marching there and then upon Glasgow.

The council correctly interpreting these actions as the signal for the outbreak of the long-expected rebellion recalled Claverhouse from the south-west to handle the situation, and by 31 May he marched from Glasgow via Rutherglen to Hamilton in search of the rebels. There he captured John King, one of the more radical of the field preachers, and fourteen Conventiclers. Pressing on to Strathaven, which he reached on 1 June, intelligence revealed a conventicle was to be held that day at Hairlawhill, two miles from Darvel in Ayrshire. But when Claverhouse finally caught up with the Conventiclers they were drawn up, not for a service, but for battle. The scene was marshy moorland known as Drumclog and to the surprise of Claverhouse the Conventiclers not only held their own but with a wild charge routed his forces with the loss of several officers and over 30 men. Flushed by their success the Coventiclers decided to press home their advantage on the following day, but, without artillery, failed dismally in their attack upon Glasgow. With the withdrawal of the government

forces on 3 June better success attended their next endeavour
and the city, on which they took their revenge for their previous
failure by burning and looting some of the houses, was for a
time occupied by the insurgents. Their main camp was, however, at Bothwell Bridge near Hamilton and they were there
joined by other conventicling stalwarts mainly drawn from the
west, but including a few drawn from the east coast. As however the army grew in size so too did the dissensions in its ranks
as the more radical Conventiclers who had initiated the rising
were joined by others of more moderate persuasion both in their
attitude to the state and their relationship with the indulged.

These differences came to a head before the battle of Bothwell Bridge in a series of declarations and counter-declarations
which were to be crucial for both presbyterianism and the
covenanting cause. With the exception of the few present who
would have agreed with Blackadder that "the Lord called for
a testimony by suffering rather than by outward deliverance",[17]
two distinct parties emerged. Of these one led by Welsh was
essentially clerical in its leadership, consisting of all but two or
at most four of the eighteen ministers present with the insurgent
army. Welsh did not wish the Indulgences to be declared unlawful until this had been done by a free General Assembly. In
a declaration affixed to the mercat cross in Hamilton this party
re-affirmed the defensive nature of the rising which they
averred had been occasioned by the woeful state of the land
and church through the brutal execution of the laws and the
refusal of redress from the magistrates. In stressing the subject's
allegiance to the magistrates, their maintenance and defence
of the king's authority, and in their desire for a free parliament
and General Assembly they accepted a degree of Erastianism
and developed an appeal to presbyterianism at large which
placed them nearer the indulged than the party which they
were destined to fight beside. Their opponents on the other
hand led by Hamilton railed against all the defections and en-
croachments upon the prerogatives of Jesus Christ and stressed
in their declarations their abhorrence of the Indulgences and
the indulged asserting that "they would sheathe their swords
as soon in them that owned the Indulgence as they would do
in any of the Malignants".[18] A king who had broken the

D

covenant, altered the polity of the church and waged war against the godly was equally to be distrusted and while they were prepared to leave the question of allegiance to his authority open, their disapproval of such power was always to the fore.

Discussion and arguments on such issues characterized three whole weeks after Drumclog. A period of respite which should have been turned to military advantage was instead utilized as an "immense conventicle of wrangling theologians".[19] Portable pulpits served as the vehicle for interminable discussions on the maintenance of the covenant against which more practical military arrangements could not prevail. Needless to say the authorities were more single minded in their purpose. If their initial policy was cautious, the weeks after Drumclog were used to build up a large and well equipped fighting force, command of which was to be given to the Duke of Monmouth, who had been commissioned if necessary to use English troops to quell the rising. On 21 June, three days after his arrival in Edinburgh, Monmouth was in command of an army of 10,000 men before Bothwell Bridge. By contrast the army which he faced was tired and dispirited and reduced at 4,000 men to half its previous size by the constant arguments. The government artillery was matched by one small cannon. Leadership amongst the conventicling army was equally at a premium and the inexplicable failure to mine the actual bridge allowed the government forces to cross in unbroken order. In the circumstances it is hardly surprising that the initial artillery bombardment broke the conventicling ranks and allowed Monmouth's cavalry quickly to turn the battle into a rout, with Hamilton himself one of the first to flee.

Losses in the actual battle were small on both sides, but whereas the government forces achieved security through their victory no such good fortune attended the vanquished. In the pursuit which followed the dragoons initially showed little mercy to those they encountered and it has been variously estimated that some two to four hundred were killed as they fled the field. The lesser of these estimates may be nearer the truth for in addition to the 1,200 Conventiclers who surrendered on the spot many others, including Kid the radical field preacher, were apprehended as they fled. Seizure, rather than slaughter, was undoubtedly the policy of Monmouth who not only restrained the dragoons from widespread pursuit but also categorically repudiated suggestions that all the prisoners should be put to death. In his actions he demonstrated most aptly the sentiment later attributed to him that "he could not kill men in cold blood that was only for butchers".[20]

In the period immediately following his victory Monmouth was equally conciliatory in his attitude. As a friend of English dissenters he showed himself equally willing to listen to presbyterian dissenters and the proclamation of a Third Indulgence, which was authorized by the king on 29 June, may be directly attributed to his influence. This edict, while continuing all laws against field conventicles, authorized house conventicles south of the Tay except within two miles of Edinburgh and within one mile of St Andrews, Glasgow and Stirling. Ministers allowed to preach under such conditions were, however, to find surety for their good behaviour, and none who had taken part in the uprising was to be licensed. Further relief followed on 11 July when all fines for ecclesiastical offences not amounting to treason were remitted and orders given for the release, on suitable caution, of all ministers not involved in the rebellion. A meaningful compromise might have been achieved if these concessions had been fully implemented. Anti-Erastianism if not dead was for the time being discredited, and the party which still maintained this attitude could no longer claim to represent the presbyterian conscience. The return of Monmouth to England five days before the receipt of these further concessions partially jeopardized this policy, but even so the terms of the Third Indulgence were re-iterated by the council on 19 September. Following upon this at least fifteen ministers found the necessary sureties and were authorized to preach. The parishes of seven of these so indulged lay in the diocese of Glasgow but the remainder lay in the diocese of St Andrews, and this extension of the area served by the indulged not only represents a significant change of emphasis in declared presbyterian support but may also have influenced the council in its virtual curtailment of this policy after December 1679.

Similar trends are discernible in the policies directed against those who had actually taken up arms against authority. Initial action following upon the battle of Bothwell Bridge was not unduly severe. Mopping-up operations, which were mainly designed to catch as many as possible of the 65 leading insurgents who had been named in a proclamation against rebels on 26 June, were mounted in various parts of the country. Claverhouse in particular was active in Ayrshire and Galloway but, though his troops were undoubtedly guilty of pillage and of exacting fines of doubtful legality from a number of conventicling sympathizers, cases of inflicting actual bodily harm were few and far between. Even the prisoners who had been taken to Edinburgh and whose ranks and been swollen to about 1,400 as further arrests were made suffered far less than has sometimes been asserted. The confinement of the majority in huts in a vacant walled-in part of what became Greyfriars' churchyard might almost be considered a better fate than imprisonment in conventional insanitary and overcrowded prisons. The season of their confinement for the majority of prisoners extended only over the summer and lack of adequate security made escape a practical possibility for a not inconsiderable number.

The large number of prisoners created a problem from the outset. Transportation of some had been seen as a possible solution almost immediately after the battle and on 29 June the king had concurred with the council's suggestion that three or four hundred of "the rabble may be transported to forraigne plantations . . . so that they never may be capable to returne for creating new disturbances".[21] The remainder, with the exception of any principal malefactors, were to be liberated after pledging themselves never to rise in arms again. The release of bonded prisoners began at the end of July and, although the council still expressed willingness on 14 August to transport three or four hundred prisoners irrespective of their willingness to subscribe, in the event all prisoners, with the exception of two field preachers John Kid and John King who had supported the more radical anti-Erastian faction at Bothwell Bridge and had been apprehended after the battle, were given the opportunity of securing their liberty. The royal indemnity was proclaimed shortly after the execution of the two preachers on 14 August and the task of liberating prisoners began almost at once. Some 400 remained obdurate and, while in the face of this resistance the attitude of the king and Lauderdale hardened to the extent that criminal proceedings were initiated on 26 August against nine men who refused to acknowledge that the rising had been a rebellion or the slaying of Archbishop Sharp was murder, the council used every device open to it to persuade the remaining prisoners to take the bond. In its efforts it was joined by several presbyterian ministers who in conference in Edinburgh declared that the bond might be lawfully subscribed. These entreaties were not altogether ineffective as another 100 of the prisoners either signed and were released unconditionally or in a few instances solved their dilemma of conscience by escape. Even after the bond had been officially withdrawn and the council had begun to make arrangements for the transportation of the recalcitrant it was authorized by the king in a letter of 1 November 1679 to admit to the bond any who might show good cause as to why they had not previously subscribed. At this point about two thirds of the remaining 300 prisoners had evidently expressed willingness to sign, but at this juncture the sectionalism which had vitiated the Conventiclers' cause before Bothwell Bridge demonstrated that it could be equally dangerous in defeat. The supplicants were immediately accused by their fellows led by Robert Garnock, a Stirling blacksmith, of defecting from the cause by acknowledging their rising to be sinful. This in turn led to a refusal to worship with the defectors, who eventually split among themselves into those who wished to sign the bond and those who were persuaded by John Blackadder to rescind their petition and stand firm against it. The resultant confusion was such that it is scarcely surprising that, with the exception of 30 prisoners who were to be tried for treason, the council decided to transport most of the remaining prisoners without further discrimination. Two hundred and fifty-eight prisoners were to be eventually packed into the holds of the ship known as *The Crown of London* which had been chartered by an Edinburgh merchant to take them to Barbados. The ship sailed after a twelve-day delay on 27 November, only to be wrecked off the Orkney coast on 10 December when all but 30 to 36 of the prisoners perished. In this unfortunate matter little culpability can perhaps be attached to the council which likewise exercised a fair amount of lenience in the one major trial which, in addition to that of Kid and King, followed the rising.

In this, 30 men, including some of these arraigned on 26 August, were initially accused of treason for failing to acknowledge that the killing of the archbishop was murder. All of them were given the opportunity of taking the bond and all but six actually subscribed. Of these one was acquitted as not being present amongst the rebels, but the remaining five were duly convicted and hanged on Magus Moor in expiation for the murder of Archbishop Sharp in whose death they had concurred only after its commission by assassins who remained at large. In so far as the number of executions fell far short of even the total hangings following the Pentland Rising the authorities cannot be accused on this score of acting vindictively towards the rebels. On the other hand 35 lairds in Dumfries and Galloway were forfeited and dispossessed, the estate of one of these, Patrick McDowall of Freuch, being bestowed upon Claverhouse, while other officers were likewise rewarded. Fines and occasionally dispossession were also inflicted upon many whose sole crime had been to remain from the muster of the militia preceding Bothwell Bridge. In those acts the council was much more exacting in its attitude. If, however, the council felt that this mixture of severity in conjunction with its conciliatory attitude to the lesser participants would finally resolve the religious controversies of the period it was quickly to realize that its difficulties were far from at an end.

Chapter Seven

THE AFTERMATH,
CAMERONIANS AND PRESBYTERIANS

THE EFFECTS OF the battle of Bothwell Bridge and its immediate aftermath were to have far reaching consequences. In political terms it meant the end of Lauderdale's administration for, though he retained the secretaryship for more than a year, he was superseded in all but name first by the Duke of Monmouth and then by the Duke of York who arrived in Scotland in November 1679 and on 4 December took his seat on the council without taking the oath. His arrival heralded the effective end to Monmouth's proposals for extended toleration and the removal of Lauderdale from office in October 1680 finally dashed any hopes for a continuance of that policy.

Lauderdale's career is not easily assessed. As a zealous upholder of royal supremacy he had been a loyal servant to Charles II who in turn showed little gratitude for past services but instead consented to his removal from practically all his offices, the secretaryship being conferred upon the Earl of Moray. In the long run the campaign organized by his many political opponents had proved successful, but it is important to remember that their opposition stemmed not so much from disapproval of his methods or disagreement with his policies but rather from envy. Lauderdale was to be dispossessed but his opponents were also his heirs and covetous of his authority. If Lauderdale's arrogance had increased with his power, if friends such as Moray and Kincardine had been alienated through the malice of his wife, his final dismissal was not because of these faults but rather through political failure. The policy of rigorous repression of conventicles in which Lauderdale had concurred had proved ineffective and armed rebellion had been the outcome. To king and Conventicler alike Lauderdale's policy had been adjudged unacceptable. Both reviled him, but it was the supremacy which he had created that allowed the king's cause to triumph in 1679, and had the presbyterian Conventiclers paused to reflect they might have fared much worse had it not been for Lauderdale's genuine concern for presbyterianism. Unable to assure its retention at the Restoration he had nevertheless initiated a policy of toleration at a period when further repression might have been expected. If the Indulgences had not been as acceptable as Lauderdale might have hoped they had contributed to the maintenance and growth of a more moderate presbyterian opinion. As long as Lauderdale remained in power that body of dissent had been little disturbed by the repressive policies aimed at Conventiclers. With his removal extremists and moderates alike were to be indiscriminately penalized in an attempt to remove all trace of schism from the church.

The opportunity to do so was undoubtedly presented by the survival of a small sect of covenanting presbyterians—the Covenanters or Cameronians, as they came to be called after their leader Richard Cameron—who, although they could no longer validly claim to represent the presbyterian viewpoint, attempted to do so in a variety of declarations. Their leader returned from Holland in October 1679 having been present there during the insurrection. Whilst there he had fallen further under the influence of MacWard and Brown, who had ordained him in the Scots Kirk in Rotterdam, and as a result he was more implacable in his opposition to the indulged than before. In Scotland, however, he found a very different mood: field conventicling had all but ceased as a result of military activity, and, while Blackadder and a few others maintained house conventicles, the only preacher prepared to follow Cameron's example was Donald Cargill. Former extremists such as Welsh refused to accept Cameron's contentions and some of the more moderate presbyterians condemned as unconstitutional the idea of an itinerant ministry conducted by a minister ordained abroad. If lay supporters of his cause were more forthcoming they were never numerous and it is therefore all the more surprising that this small sect of covenanting presbyterians and their martyrs has subsequently been taken to represent dissent in the decade following Bothwell Bridge.

That this has been so undoubtedly sprang from their in-
tensity of conviction expressed in a variety of manifestoes which
not only explained their tenets but also strengthened government resolution that such dangerous men must be extirpated.
A paper discovered on Henry Hall of Haughhead when he
and Cargill, who escaped, were accosted at Queensferry
sparked off this reaction, for not only were the king and council
abjured but signatories were to be bound to the overthrow of
their power. The government of the revitalized church was to
be presbyterian and free from all state control, but authority
within the church was to rest only with the godly "to be exercised
not after a carnal manner by the plurality of votes, or authority
of a single person, but according to the word of God; so that
the word makes and carries the sentence and not plurality of
votes".[1] If the sentiments expressed in the Queensferry Paper
had not been sufficient to alarm the council the proclamation
on 22 June by Cameron and twenty of his associates of an even
more extreme declaration at the cross of Sanquhar convinced
it that resolute action was required. In this further manifesto
its adherents "as the representatives of the true presbyterian
kirk and covenanted nation of Scotland" solemnly disowned
their king and declared "war with such a tyrant and usurper
and the men of his practices, as enemies to our Lord Jesus
Christ, and his cause and covenants".[2] Reaction was swift, a
price was placed upon the lives of Cameron, Cargill and their
associates. Apprised of Cameron's movements by the indulged
minister of Ochiltree, a party of dragoons caught up with
Cameron and about 60 of his associates at Aird's Moss. In the
ensuing skirmish the troopers suffered more losses than their
opponents, but, as Cameron and his brother Michael both fell
in the struggle and Hackston of Rathillet was captured and
later executed, the Cameronian cause suffered a heavy blow.
Cargill was now the sole remaining field-preacher and after
he excommunicated the king, the dukes of York and Monmouth and the leading Scottish politicians at Torwood in
Stirlingshire in September 1680, the search for him and other
Cameronian adherents was intensified. In addition to Hackston, two of the other prisoners taken at Aird's Moss were
executed, and they were followed to the gallows by at least

eleven other adherents of Cargill or Cameron. Among their
number were two women, Isobel Alison of Perth and Marion
Harvey of Bo'ness, but others were more fortunate; three
women who had been actually present at the Torwood conventicle were liberated with no more than the threat of a
scourging if they were found at conventicles again. For Cargill,
however, there could be no respite and after he was apprehended with two companions at Covington on 12 July 1681 his
fate was sealed; he with his two companions and two other
Conventiclers being hanged and dismembered on 27 July.
Five further executions were carried out in October, Robert
Garnock from Stirling who had urged non-acceptance of the
bond by prisoners after Bothwell Bridge being amongst this
number. Most of those hanged could have saved themselves
by acknowledging the authority of the king, but this they
resolutely refused to do. In addition they repudiated all
ministers other than Cargill, and in this last extremity the
"Remnant" finally separated themselves from the main body
of presbyterian dissent.

   The exclusive claims of the Cameronians, hardly surprisingly,
prompted others to follow even stranger paths. Pre-eminent
among these were the Gibbites or Sweet Singers, followers of
John Gibb, a shipmaster of Bo'ness who persuaded three men
and 26 women to renounce a wicked world and to follow him
into the wilderness of the Pentland hills. There they spent their
time fasting, praying and singing psalms. The ways of the
world were totally renounced, so too were the covenants,
metrical psalms, the translation of both Testaments, the
division into chapters and verses and even the table of contents.
All authority throughout the world was also condemned in
their declaration that "there is none in the Kingdom . . . that
we can converse with as Christians".[3] In the very outrageous-
ness of their beliefs, however, lay their safety for, when they
too were apprehended as ambulatory Conventiclers, the Duke
of York declared his amusement at their beliefs and they were
all eventually released from their imprisonment on renouncing
disloyal principles and giving bail. All but Gibb and three of
the others, who were eventually transported to America,
appear to have complied with these conditions in an incident

which provides an interesting contrast to the case of the Cameronians who continued to be persecuted long after any real threat from the sect had vanished.

Persecution was not exclusively reserved for Cameronians, however, and it would appear that where it suited the government found it convenient to treat Cameronians and other presbyterians who neither approved nor countenanced the extremists as part and parcel of a single problem. With the effective curtailment of field conventicles house meetings became the special object of the council's concern. In May 1680 it was decreed that no house conventicles should be held and no meeting places erected within a mile of any parish church which had a regular incumbent; that dissenting ministers should not be allowed to meet in presbyteries and that no such ministers should be licensed within twelve miles of Edinburgh. This decree which virtually withdrew the privileges offered in the Third Indulgence stemmed from a petition of the bishops and in particular at the request of Alexander Burnet who had been translated from Glasgow to St Andrews after the death of Archbishop Sharp. An implacable opponent of the policy of conciliation his advancement at this time was a prime factor in the maintenance of repression. Conventiclers were brought before the council with unfailing regularity, while at the same time action against indulged ministers was stepped up. As a result all but one of the licences granted under the Third Indulgence had been recalled by 6 November 1680. In the following year the process of withdrawing concessions from indulged ministers continued and among those prosecuted were John Hutchison indulged at Dundonald, James Veitch at Mauchline and Robert Miller at Ochiltree who received scant reward for his co-operation with the authorities in their efforts to track down Cameron. Many of the ministers so arraigned, whether deprived or indulged, chose to go into exile in England at this period. John Welsh who had fled south after Bothwell Bridge had died there in January 1681 and other preachers, such as Gabriel Semple who was apprehended in July of that year and James Fraser of Brae who was imprisoned for a time in Blackness castle, decided that they could no longer remain in Scotland. Their former

associate John Blackadder was less fortunate in this respect for
after his apprehension in Edinburgh on 5 April 1681 he was
despatched without delay to the Bass where he was to remain
until his death almost five years later. With the removal of one
of the few remaining field preachers and the success which was
apparently meeting their efforts to suppress Cameronians and
presbyterians alike the council at the close of 1681 must have
been more confident than ever before that the problem of
dissent was almost resolved.

Any hopes in this direction, however, had been already unwittingly shattered by two acts passed in parliament on 13
August 1681. The first of these—a succession act—in securing
the right of hereditary succession ensured that James, Duke of
York, would succeed his brother Charles while the second
—a Test act—required office holders to swear that they held
the protestant faith as expressed in the Scots Confession of 1560
and recognized the king as supreme in all causes temporal and
spiritual. The allusion to the Scots Confession was only inserted after a long debate on the motion of Sir James Dalrymple
who had possibly hoped that this addition might cause the
measure to be rejected. But few apparently knew the text of
the Confession which contained statements totally at variance
with the substance of the oath as that Christ is "the only Head
of his kirk" and that the sovereign was only to be obeyed in
matters "not repugning to the commandment of God".[4]
Difficulties were at once raised, not only was the recognition
of the king's supremacy inconsistent with the Scots Confession,
but the Test Act taken in conjunction with the earlier Act of
Succession involved the eventual acceptance of a catholic
sovereign as supreme governor of the church. Even ministers
who had loyally supported the established church throughout
all its previous difficulties found this a bitter pill to swallow.
The ultra-conservative synod of Aberdeen was constrained to
issue an explanation of the meaning of the Test Act after
ministers had stated their objections to it. Among other things
this explication reserved intrinsic spiritual power, permitted
meetings for church discipline and for the protection of
protestantism; and admitted the possibility of alteration of
church government when not accomplished by arms or sedition.

A similar declaration of intent was issued by the synod of Dunkeld, and in the face of such protests the council felt it wise to issue their own interpretation on 3 November 1681. In this it was enacted that ministers who took the Test need not swear to every proposition or clause contained in the Confession "but only to the true protestant religion, founded on the word of God . . . as it is opposit to poperie and phanatisisme".[5] This concession which was in itself inconsistent with the declaration in the Test that it was taken "in the plain genuine sense and meaning of the words, without any equivocation, mental reservation, or any manner of evasion whatsoever" was accompanied by the threat that refusers of the oath should be "esteemed persons disaffected to the protestant religion, and to his majesty's government".[6]

No amount of explanations and concessions could persuade some of the validity of the Test Act. Among the ministers who refused the Test, the most notable was Laurence Charteris, professor of divinity at Edinburgh University, and his example was followed by a considerable number of other ministers who were consequently deprived. Estimates of the total number deposed have varied between 30 and 80. Many of these deprived were from the Lothians, and Paterson, Bishop of Edinburgh, stated in February 1683 that there were more recusants in the two contiguous presbyteries of Haddington and Dalkeith than in all the rest of Scotland. At least seventeen ministers were ousted in these presbyteries and if accurate this would favour the lesser of the two estimates, but this is probably a conservative figure and the final count may have been nearer 50. Whatever the figure, the church had suffered another serious defection at a time when unity seemed more than a remote possibility. The secession from the established church of a group of moderate ministers inevitably added a new dimension to the dissenters' cause. Although about twenty followed the example of Gilbert Burnet and entered the Church of England, others acceded to non-conformity. Indeed, although it may be concluded that repression had broken the covenanting movement as such, it would be unwise to assume that "the main body of presbyterian dissent" had been similarly affected.[7] It may even be argued that in the breaking of the radical Covenanters, the moderate presbyterians gained in strength. Added to the presbyterians still uneasily contained in the official church and to the indulged still actively ministering outwith it there was also the vast majority of those who in person or in spirit had supported the insurgents of 1679. The implementation of the Test Act brought further lay and clerical adherents to a cause which could convincingly associate itself with the defence of protestantism within the realm.

Objections to the Test Act were by no means confined to ministers. Several members of the council including Lord President Dalrymple, Lord Clerk-Register Murray and the Earl of Argyll refused to subscribe. Dalrymple was forced into exile in Holland soon to be joined by Argyll who, although eventually subscribing, added the caveat that he only did so "as far as it is consistent with itself and the Protestant Religion".[8] For this he was deprived of his seat on the council and his commissionership of the treasury, was eventually tried and found guilty of treason, escaping however before the inevitable sentence was pronounced. Other members of the nobility, including the duke of Hamilton and earls of Haddington, Nithsdale, Cassillis and Sutherland followed Argyll's example by refusing to subscribe and, although they did not suffer his fate, which can be largely attributed to personal vindictiveness against the Campbells, their action dictated an eventual reshaping of the whole administration.

At this stage, however, the Duke of York still held full sway and it was in accord with his policy that pressure upon nonconformists was maintained during the early part of 1682. In this respect the excuse, if such was required, for an increasingly active policy of repression had been provided by the Cameronians. In practice, the "Remnant" should no longer have been regarded as an active opposition as their congregations which lacked ministers after the arrest and execution of Cargill had become no more than a group of praying societies. But in their anxiety to maintain links with one another, a Union or General Correspondence of these societies had been mooted and this body held its first convention at Lesmahagow on 15 December 1681. Arrangements were made for the transmission of a circular letter every fortnight and for the holding of quarterly meetings the first of which was to be held on 15 March 1682. On a less wise note the convention resolved to have a declaration published at Lanark on 12 January 1682. This was duly effected, 40 horsemen and 20 men on foot attending the reading of the declaration which homologated the Declarations of Rutherglen and Sanquhar and repudiated all unconstitutional acts of the king. Although this was undoubtedly provocative the council would have been well advised to ignore an act which, with a limited number of adherents and little ability to match their resolutions with action, was no more realistic than the advocation of psalm singing as an answer to the world's problems by the Gibbites. With the Cameronians leaderless and totally rejected, even by their fellow presbyterians, further persecution was pointless and cruel, but it was nevertheless relentlessly pursued by the council, which also seized upon the opportunity to deal with the general problem of dissent.

One of its chief instruments in this work was Claverhouse who was commissioned as sheriff of Wigtown, in place of Sir Andrew Agnew who had refused the Test, and, as sheriff-depute of the stewartries of Kirkcudbright and Annandale and county of Dumfries, had his remit extended to these districts on 31 January. His instructions were personally to prosecute all persons, other than heritors, who were implicated in the 1679 rebellion and who had refused or failed to take the bond required for indemnity or, having subscribed, had broken their pledge by either attending conventicles or failing to attend their parish church. In the initial stages of his campaign Claverhouse tempered severity with mercy, but those who had failed to take the bond for one reason or another were relentlessly pursued, soldiers quartered on their lands, their houses pillaged and their families reduced to near starvation. In his own words he "rifled so their houses, ruined their goods . . . that their wyfes and schildring were broght to sterving".[9] His sweep of the countryside was so efficient that few eluded the net of Claverhouse and his force of specially enlisted roughriders who scoured the district by day and by night. By the end of March the number of heritors who had been apprehended was sufficient to justify their conveyance to Edinburgh where the majority were liberated on taking the bond or subscribing the Test. Only a few such as Joseph Learmont, one of the principals in the Pentland Rising, remained obdurate and were commited to the Bass. No such pressure was required to coerce the lesser offenders as in their case direct threat of further and immediate penalties was sufficient to fill the parish churches again, congregations dramatically increasing and in some cases rising from a mere handful of worshippers to attendances of several hundred. By 1 April Claverhouse could boast that this "contry nou is in parfait peace".[10] The conformity was undoubtedly more apparent than real, however, but there is little doubt that the council's determination as a result of this success led to the hope that intervention authorized on similar lines elsewhere would produce equal dividends. During the month of March similar commissions were authorized in the shires of Haddington, Kinross, Perth and West Lothian. Apparent success attended many of these efforts, and ostensible progress is suggested by reports similar to that of Sir William Bruce from the shire of Kinross "that he had convened before him all who were present at the late conventicles, and fined them, and since, they have all, save a few, returned to their duty, and engaged to keep their parish kirk".[11] On the other hand, Coventiclers in Ayrshire and Lanarkshire proved to be much less tractable in their attitudes and even Claverhouse, flushed with his success in Galloway, found that the help which he accorded Dalyell in these shires met with only limited response. Such operations had, moreover, to be repeated at fairly regular intervals and in disparate parts of the country, a fact in itself which did not make the council's task any easier.

In the circumstances of these commissions, it was inevitable that occasional brutalities should result. Cases such as that of the two Nisbet boys, aged ten and fourteen, who were brutally beaten by dragoons in an effort to make them reveal their father's whereabouts, and of a fifteen-year-old boy in New Monkland who was tormented and tortured by a callous officer in the hope that he would betray his master, are commonplace occurrences in any military occupation. But these cases were isolated incidents and far more widespread suffering was probably caused by the myriad of petty tyrants

who under these commissions and others were authorized to
proceed against all who had associated with rebels and absented
themselves from their parish church. Nowhere is this more
clearly illustrated than in the regality court of Melrose in which
the bailie, George Pringle of Blindlie, relentlessly fined those
within his jurisdiction "who have transgressed the acts of
Parliament forbidding the frequenting of house and field conventicles, and keeping disorderly baptisms and marriages, and
withdrawing from their own parish churches".[12] A few of the
accused such as Alexander Scott of Blainslie who was accused
of favouring William Spotiswood in Blainslie "ane declaired
rebell and fugitive . . . who was allwayes in armes in company
with the rebells and was constant precentor to the haill field
meittings" may be adjudged to have been sympathetic towards
those who had challenged the authority of the state.[13] But the
vast majority of those fined in this court, some on more than
one occasion, were simple presbyterian non-conformists who
were being harried for their religious rather than their political
persuasion.

This became increasingly true as the council re-doubled its
efforts in all parts of the country. The Cameronian remnant
became increasingly ineffective as time went on, and although
they continued to hold their quarterly meetings, one being held
at Talla Linn in Tweedsmuir on 15 June 1682, they only
served to reveal further divisions in their ranks. Their compara-
tive inactivity at this time may explain why in the period before
the departure of the Duke of York in May 1682 only one
capital sentence was inflicted in the midst of this wave of more
general religious persecution. This was in the case of William
Harvey who had participated in the proclamation of a declaration at Lanark in 1679 and had been present at Bothwell
Bridge. Despite his willingness to recognize the king in his
lawful authority and even say "God Save the King",[14] he was
executed at Lanark on 2 March as a retaliatory measure for
the Cameronian action there earlier in the year. Others who
were brought to trial such as Christian Fyfe who railed against
bishops and four Galloway rebels Maclellan of Barscobe,
Macklewraith of Auchinfloor, Fleming of Auchinfin and
Joseph Learmont were all sentenced to death but reprieved,

In these reprieves the Duke of York concurred and it is possibly not without significance that his return to England in May 1682 was followed by increasing severity in sentences demanded by the council.

The reshaping of the administration shortly before the duke's return may also have contributed to this end. More moderate councillors had been ousted after their refusal to take the Test and the majority of council members thereafter were implacable opponents of religious or political dissent. The new chancellor, Sir George Gordon, afterwards first Earl of Aberdeen, was an ardent royalist and a willing supporter of the Duke of York's cause. William Douglas, Earl of Queensberry, created marquis in May 1682 and duke in February 1684, was, as his advancement in honours would suggest, equally devoted to the royal cause in his post as treasurer. This loyal band was increased by the appointment of the Earl of Perth as Justice-General and Earl of Middleton as conjoint secretary of state with the Earl of Moray. In their hands the duke's final recommendation that "a steady procedure might be taken to suppress the rebellious persons not yet reduced to their obedience, especially in the shires of Cliddisdaill, Teviotdale, Fyfe and Air, and that some of the troupes might be sent to these places" was to be resolutely implemented.[15]

In the second half of the year repression was not only maintained but extended. Commissions of justiciary continued to be granted with increasing regularity, wide powers being granted to Major White for the sheriffdom of Ayr and to Adam Urquhart of Meldrum for the shires of Haddington, Selkirk, Berwick and Peebles on 3 August 1682. As these show, the problem of dissenters was far from resolved and was as pressing in the east as the west. Before the end of the year, such a commission was also to be found necessary in Ross and Cromarty in which conventicling had never entirely ceased. The major targets continued to be non-conformists untainted with rebellion and the policies of quartering and fining remained the standard means of enforcing compliance to the established church. Nevertheless before the end of the year it became apparent that if such threats proved ineffective, sterner measures still might be enforced.

The execution of Robert Gray, a Northumbrian, who had disowned the king's authority and disowned the Test on 19 May and that of Thomas Lauchlan who had been present at Bothwell Bridge on 16 August, if scarcely indicative of a marked change of policy nevertheless suggested a precedent for future action. In Gray's case his repudiation of the Test was an important factor in the prosecution's case while in that of Lauchlan an old charge and former sentence of death were revived against one whose more recent offences were not recounted. By the end of the year attitudes had hardened even further and, although reprieves were granted to two Galloway landowners who had been found guilty on somewhat uncertain evidence of being present at Bothwell Bridge, three Cameronians were executed on 15 December. If their conviction and sentence for treason were legally justified, the proof offered against Alexander Home, who was hanged on 21 December, was much less convincing. The integrity of the judicial bench which had been in doubt since 1677, when the king insisted that all commissions should depend on good behaviour, had now under the new Justice-General Perth reached the point where the judicature was no longer motivated by legal principles but rather by practical political considerations.

Such considerations led to an escalation of repressive measures. The year 1683 was characterized by a host of repressive rules and regulations designed to bring the most recalcitrant of Conventiclers to task. A persistent effort was also expended on ensuring that local magistrates enforced the laws in all their severity and were not in collusion with those who appeared before them. In this respect the magistrates of Linlithgow were obliged to report to the council on 4 January on their diligence in suppressing malcontents, but their reply while deemed satisfactory did little to suppress religious dissidence in the burgh or contiguous shire. In attempting to deal with a similar problem in Lanark, Sir John Harper of Cambusnethan, sheriff-depute of that county, was imprisoned in Edinburgh castle on 27 January and not released until April. On 27 February Cromwell Lockhart of Lee was appointed provost of the burgh of Lanark with power to appoint new magistrates as many of the previous holders of that office were themselves in prison, but despite these efforts both town and district remained centres of disaffection. Commissions for the suppression of religious disaffection throughout the southern shires continued to be appointed, while on 27 March the shire of Nairn was included with Ross and Cromarty as an area in which persons were held to be guilty of "withdrawing from the publick ordinances in their owne paroch kirks".[16]

In the circumstances the council reacted by enforcing the existing laws with the utmost severity and finding these not severe enough devised new measures to which more rigorous penalties might be attached. For some, however, existing penalties were severe enough as the execution of the Cameronian John Nisbet in Kilmarnock on 4 April amply demonstrated. Nine days later, however, the net was to be widened by a proclamation authorizing the council and its deputies to call before them all persons suspected of having harboured rebels, whether by accident or design, and whether or not the rebels had been denounced as such. None the less a pardon was to be offered to all recusants who subscribed to the Test before 1 August 1683, and for this purpose, as well as for punishing those who refused to conform, circuit courts were to be held at Edinburgh, Glasgow, Stirling, Jedburgh and Ayr.

This circuit court presided over by Perth as Justice-General and before which prosecutions were conducted by Sir George MacKenzie, the Lord Advocate, commenced its task in Stirling on 5 June 1683. Procedure was simple. All who were called were obliged to take the Test, refusal meant apprehension and compearance in Edinburgh at a later date. Although some failed to answer their summons, few of those who attended refused the Test but one who did, William Bogue of Auchinreoch, found that in his case trial for treason was to be immediate. Despite a change of heart on the matter of the Test he was to be hanged on 13 June. Bogue was undoubtedly sacrificed as an example to others. Claverhouse justified his execution to the chancellor Aberdeen, who was considering a reprieve, on the grounds that when one dies "justly for his owen faults, and may sawe a hondred to fall in the lyk, I have no scrupull".[17] The council concurred with this sentiment and Bogue was taken to Glasgow since "it was thought that the execution would be more terrible at Glasgow".[18] The effective-ness of such a sentence as the final deterrent which would bring the Conventiclers to heel was already commending itself to the council, which had concurred in two earlier executions in May and was now openly proclaimed by the justiciary who ordered "the gallowes to stand, for the better instruction of the great number of rebels who are cited to appeir".[19] A further practical demonstration of the power of the law was in fact provided on the following day when John MacQuharrie and John Smith were hanged in the belief that they had assisted in the escape of a Conventicler from his escort at Inchbelly bridge near Kilsyth six days previously. Shots had been fired and a guardsman killed, but direct proof of their involvement was certainly lacking, and they were convicted without being given the opportunity of subscribing to the Test, on the grounds that they had fought at Bothwell, burned the Test at Lanark, and called the king a tyrant.

These grim warnings of sterner punishments ahead ostensibly served their purpose and as the circuit court moved from Glasgow to Ayr, Dumfries and Jedburgh before returning to Edinburgh, those who appeared before it became increasingly pliant. This continued to be the case in Edinburgh although four further deaths were exacted before the end of a year in which the number of executions exceeded those which had followed the battle of Bothwell Bridge. One of these hanged in July was Andrew Guillan, who was executed for his part in the murder of Archbishop Sharp, but if the case against him and possibly those against Smith and MacQuharrie were criminally competent the other seven convicted, including three men hanged in December, were essentially the victims of religious persecution clothed in the legal guise of a judicial campaign directed against avowed rebels.

This campaign was to gain momentum as the extended date of 1 March 1684, up to which the indemnifying Test could be subscribed, approached. Papers found in the possession of the captured Alexander Gordon of Earlston, who was apprehended on his way to Holland in June 1683, revealed that the Camer-onians not only held "meitings who keep life in their shizme" but that they were also in touch with malcontents in the Low

Countries;[20] and the council's alarm turned to fear when James Renwick returned as an ordained minister to the "Remnant" in September 1683. Field conventicling revived and with it the spectre of a further rebellion. Government measures reflect this concern. On 3 January 1684 new commissions were granted giving full justiciary power to "cause sentence be pronounced and justice done on them accordingly" for the shires of Dumbarton, Lanark, Dumfries, Kirkcudbright and Wigtown and in the following month similar commissions were conceded for Ayrshire and Renfrewshire.[21] The levying of large fines followed the implementation of these powers. In the meanwhile the Court of Justiciary became even more assiduous in the trial of prisoners adjudged unwilling to acknowledge the king's authority, some of whom had lain in prison for years. In consequence twelve prisoners, including Captain John Paton who had fought at Rullion Green and Bothwell Bridge, were executed in the first six months of the year. Many others were transported to Carolina in the same period, thus relieving the pressure upon the prisons which in places such as Dumfries were full and overflowing with recusants. Most, if not all, of these deported in this manner were of lowly status and fining and quartering remained the standard penalty for those of substance. Justice was notably absent in many of these proceedings and was certainly seen to be lacking in the trial of Sir Hugh Campbell of Cessnock. In this case Lord Advocate MacKenzie even promised conviction before trial on charges which had eventually to be reduced to one, namely that the accused had incited rebellion by chiding fugitives from Bothwell Bridge for their cowardice. Even this charge could not be proven when MacKenzie's two suborned witnesses refused to testify. Despite acquittal Cessnock was not immediately freed, and when subsequently liberated was harried, forfeited and eventually sent to the Bass. Yet Cessnock's only crime appears to have been his presbyterianism and his attitude towards the rebels and other extreme Conventiclers had been one of disapproval. Others of equal and even greater social standing such as Sir John Pollok, Sir John Cochrane, George Lord Melville and the Earl of Loudon, were also charged at this time and it is evident that the general extirpation of presbyterianism had become paramount. Claverhouse, one of the principal agents of this policy, certainly saw this as his allotted task when in a letter to Queensberry on 19 May 1684 he wrote: "I may cur people guilty of that plaigue of presbytry be conversing with them, but can not be infected, and I see very little of that amongst those persons but may be easily rubed of".[22] Claverhouse's optimism was, however, misplaced and the cure which he and the council sought for the presbyterian plague remained for the time beyond their grasp.

The Cameronians and their minister James Renwick remained equally elusive despite a proclamation on 22 July calling on anyone to seize them. It was feared that their small field conventicles might become the focal point of a new rebellion, and to many that fear became a reality when only a week later a party of prisoners and their military escort en route from Dumfries to Edinburgh were ambushed in Enterkin pass, Dumfriesshire, and some of the prisoners rescued after a struggle in which several on both sides were killed. Retribution was swift: five of the rescuers who had been apprehended by Claverhouse on 9 August near Dumfries were tried with another Conventicler six days later in Edinburgh, and were hanged on the afternoon of their conviction. Though their punishment may have been merited, the speed of their despatch, which was in accord with a recommendation of the council on 1 August that justices proceed and pronounce sentence of death against rebels immediately, "which sentence they are to cause be execute within sex hours aftir prununceing thereof",[23] savoured of a court martial rather than trial and sentence by due process of law. The step from procedures of this nature to those of an even more summary nature was but a short one; the "killing times" had commenced.

Chapter Eight

THE KILLING TIMES

In the months which followed the execution of the Enterkin rescuers efforts were redoubled to curb the dissident. Two further executions characterized August, and the death in the same month of Archbishop Burnet of St Andrews, one of the chief exponents of repression, in no way eased the general situation. On 6 September 1684 four circuit justiciary courts were authorized to proceed against all recusants who would not take the oath of allegiance. If offenders refused, the courts were authorized "to put in executione the power of justiciary . . . with all rigour, by useing fyre and sword".[1] In September and October these courts sitting in various parts of southern Scotland vigorously followed their remit. Many submitted to the oath, condemned Conventiclers and offered to pay cess, but over a thousand refused to perjure themselves and so retain their liberty. The tolbooths of the burghs in which the circuit court sat could not house the prisoners who were thus apprehended and transportation to the plantations was increasingly regarded as a practical necessity if the inhuman conditions already prevailing in most prisons were not to become intolerable. There was, however, no respite on this score, and as the search for the disaffected intensified, it must have become apparent that few if any would eventually escape the clutches of the authorities. This realization coupled with a proclamation of 16 September declaring Renwick, who had been tried in his absence, a traitor, rebel and outlaw almost certainly drove the Remnant to further open defiance.

To this end, the Convention of Societies decided to issue a declaration, which after some hesitation was accepted by Renwick on 28 October and published by being affixed to market crosses and church doors on 8 November. In this *Apologetical Declaration and Admonitory Vindication of the True Presbyterians of the Church of Scotland*, the Cameronians reiterated

their resolution to maintain the covenants and declared that
whosoever stretch forth their hands against them whether it be
judges, soldiers or "viperous and malicious bishops and curates
. . . shall be reputed by us enemies to God and the covenanted
work of Reformation, and punished as such, according to our
power and the degree of their offence".[2] This was in effect an
open declaration of war and, when on the night of 19–20
November two soldiers were murdered after leaving a tavern at
Swyne Abbey in West Lothian, hostilities were deemed to have
commenced. On 22 November the council resolved that who-
ever owned or refused to disown the declaration should be
immediately put to death, provided that two witnesses were
present, by person or persons commissioned by the council. If
some semblance of respect for the due processes of law re-
appeared in the actual instructions issued and despatched to
West Lothian on the following day, in so far as those who
refused only to disown it were to be tried by a jury, this safeguard was jeopardized by the framing of the actual abjuration
oath on 25 November. Thereafter failure to take this oath
could mean summary execution and few, if any, were willing
to query the legal niceties involved.

Little time was wasted in making the new policies effective,
while the courts for their part stepped up judicial processes
against suspected sympathizers of the declaration by sentencing
another seven men to the gallows by the year's end. The power
of such a deterrent had little effect, however, on men who were
determined to meet violence with violence. The assassination
of the minister of Carsphairn, whether by accident or design
in December 1684, had been preceded in the previous month
by a mass attack on the prison at Kirkcudbright in which a
sentry had been killed and prisoners released, and was followed
on 18 December by a skirmish between eight armed fugitives
and mounted horse in which at least half the fugitives were
killed and two others captured and subsequently executed. As
little short of a state of war existed at this time the action of the
authorities was clearly justified, and in the case of the murderers
of the minister of Carsphairn even Renwick and his fellow
Cameronians expelled those guilty from their communion on
the grounds that their action had been initiated without proper

deliberation "in a rash and not in a Christian manner".[3] But, if action against such opponents was justifiable, the increasingly indiscriminate persecution of presbyterians who neither approved of nor countenanced the extremists was markedly less so.

Presbyterians as distinct from Cameronians were seldom executed, but their treatment was exceedingly harsh and increasingly so by 1684. The arrival of Renwick and the revival of field preaching in 1683 had been the occasion of further efforts against the presbyterians as such, and as a result the presbyterian ministers, looking to the consequences of his mission and in particular to the greater severity practised against themselves, denounced Renwick as "the great cause and occasion of all the troubles of the country".[4] Pressure on the indulged ministers was increased and the former policy was totally reversed on 27 November 1684 when the council embarked on the process of deposing all the indulged ministers because they had "brocken and transgressed" their instructions, and some of them who would not promise that they would exercise no part of their ministerial function were imprisoned in local tolbooths or sent to the Bass.[5] Thereafter all presbyterians, whatever their degree of acquiescence in the principle of state control in ecclesiastical affairs, were to be indiscriminately persecuted. Coercion had replaced convenience as the chief *raison d'être* of the established church

Many of good social standing were amongst those harmed for their adherence to presbyterianism. Twenty-six heritors in Roxburghshire alone were fined £274,237 Scots for nonchurchgoing; Sir John Maxwell of Pollok was ordered to pay £8,000 sterling with a remission of £3,000 if paid before 1 January; Zacharias Maxwell of Blawarthill was imprisoned for life and also fined 20,000 merks. These were but a few of the many in this class who similarly suffered. Only one, however, was obliged to pay a higher penalty. This was demanded of Robert Baillie of Jerviswood, scholar and scientist, who was as much disliked for his political as his ecclesiastical principles. Indeed at his trial on 23 December it was the charge of conspiring to overthrow the government and debar York from the succession which led him to the gallows, but it is equally clear

that his sympathies with the deprived ministers and earlier
brushes with the authorities in this respect had made him a
marked man. Even before the execution of Baillie, the campaign
against presbyterianism was beginning to pay dividends.
Parishioners, however reluctantly, were returning to their
parish churches if only for fear of being mistaken for fanatical
separatists. None the less many still remained obdurate and in
such cases the device of fining the heritors and transporting the
poor continued unabated throughout 1685. If, in many cases,
transportation was seen as the final solution for obdurate
presbyterians it nevertheless took time to effect. In the meantime the prisons grew more crowded, and it was in order to
relieve this problem that the council resolved to utilize Dunnottar castle as a state prison. To this grim stronghold, near
Stonehaven, situated on a bleak headland rising from the sea
on cliffs 160 feet high, 274 prisoners were despatched from
Edinburgh and Leith on 18 May 1685. Some were, however,
found unfit to travel, others decided to take the oath, and
seventeen escaped in transit. None the less over 150 prisoners,
including three ministers, arrived at Dunnottar on 24 May.
There they were packed into two vaults, the conditions in which
are described in a petition for an alleviation of the prisoners'
lot by the wives of two of them. One hundred and ten men and
women were in one vault:

> where there is litle or no daylight at all, and contrarie to all
> modestie, men and women promiscuouslie togither, and
> fourtie and two more in another roume in the same condition,
> and no person allowed to come near them with meat or
> drink, but such bread and drink as scarce any rationall
> creature can live upon, and yet at extraordinary rates, being
> twentie pennies each pynt of ale, which is not worth a plack
> the pint, and the peck of sandie dustie meal is offered to
> them at eighteen shillings per peck. And not so much as a
> drink of water allowed to be caryed to them, whereby they
> are not only in a starving condition, but must inevitably
> incurr a plague or other fearful diseases.[6]

The council ordered that conditions should be improved, but
little appears to have been achieved towards this end. It was

in these vaults rather than on the scaffold or in the fields that the dissenting presbyterians suffered, not because they were traitors, but as religious non-conformists.

So too the large number of prisoners who were banished during the year. Many of the prisoners in Dunnottar were eventually disposed of in this manner, being joined by others who had been apprehended after the Argyll rising. Nearly 100 men and women, of whom 70 perished on the voyage, sailed from Leith on 5 September 1685. Smaller consignments left at regular intervals, some of these heading for voluntary exile in a small Scottish settlement in East New Jersey which had been founded by the Quaker, Robert Barclay of Urie in Aberdeenshire. As convicts or exiles the journey ahead was arduous and uncertain, and, while some made a new life for themselves many died in transit or in bondage. From these persecutions and others which involved branding, cutting in the ear or simple neglect in prison there was to be little respite until the policy of Indulgence was revived in 1687.

The success of the campaign against the presbyterians had largely rested on the harsh measures which had been introduced to meet the threat of the resurgent Cameronians. In their case, however, there could be no question of successfully harrying the "Remnant" back into the fold of the established church. Even their fellow presbyterians were unacceptable to the Cameronians who would accept no one but Renwick as their minister. In their case extirpation alone could maintain the unity of the established church. To this end the council published a further proclamation denouncing the declaration on 30 December 1684 and ordering its upholders to be "executed to the death".[7] In order that these might be identified everyone living south of the Tay was to assemble to take the oath renouncing the declaration. In early 1685 steps were taken to implement this decision with an order on 9 January that burghal magistrates were to exact the oath. In each parish the oath was to be taken separately "on a large sheet of paper".[8] On the same date judicial commissions were issued for eleven counties in order to effect punishment on non-jurors. In these areas the commissioners and military effectively took over the dispensation of justice. Their mode of operation varied: some of those apprehended were arbitrarily shot if they refused the oath; others appear to have been afforded some time to re- consider their position and only executed if they remained obdurate; others again appear to have been afforded some form of trial before sentence was effected. The case of eight men apprehended at Lochenkit in the parish of Urr demonstrates several of these features as four of the prisoners were summarily shot and the remaining four were taken to Grierson of Lag, apparently with a view to holding an assize if they again refused the oath. Lag, however, took their further refusal as sufficient and hanged two of them at Irongray, the others being trans- ported. In most instances failure to take the oath of abjuration was sufficient, although in the cases of John Park and James Algie, joint tenants of a farm at Eastwood in Renfrewshire, willingness to take the oath did not save them from execution at Paisley on 3 February when the commissioners discovered during the course of their trial that the accused had scruples about accepting the Test.

Three days after their execution Charles II died and was succeeded by James, Duke of York, who unlike his brother had first-hand knowledge of the situation in Scotland. A proclama- tion of indemnity issued by James shortly after accession which appeared to point towards greater leniency was, however, so restrictive in terms—it was confined to persons under the rank of property holders and exempted vagrant preachers, persons under sentence of fining and the murderers of Sharp and others—that few benefited from it especially since pardoned fugitives were to take the oath of allegiance or agree to leave the country. The renewal of the former commissions was much more significant and allowed the "killing times" to proceed with the minimum amount of dislocation. The pattern of arbitrary executions leavened with others of a more judicial nature continued through March and April, at the end of which a fresh commission was given on 21 April to Lieutenant- General Drummond "for pursueing, suppressing, and utterly destroying all such fugitive rebels as resist and disturb the peace and quiet of his majesties government".[9] Much of this concern stemmed from the inability of the commissioners to apprehend Renwick who was still actively holding field conventicles under the protection of armed guards. Another field preacher, Alexander Peden, who had been imprisoned in the Bass from 1674 to 1678 and had only then escaped transportation and obtained his release through a mix-up in London, was also still active, although not a Cameronian. The success of both men in eluding capture not only posed serious questions about the thoroughness of the military operation but also demonstrated that support for both the Cameronian and presbyterian causes was far from extinguished.

Such considerations may have led to punishments becoming more arbitrary as final success continued to elude the commissioners. On 1 May 1684 Claverhouse personally shot John Brown of Priestshiel, near Muirkirk, who had harboured Peden and refused the abjuration oath. Although the execution was justified in terms of the law, as were the other eight or nine similar cases in which he was involved, Claverhouse's account of the affair: "I caused shoot him dead, which he suffered very inconcernedly" demonstrates an insensitivity amounting to callousness.[10] If Claverhouse does not entirely deserve his "bloody" epithet, some of his associates in other parts of the country may lay claim to his title. Principal amongst these is Sir Robert Grierson of Lag who had refused an assize to four of the men apprehended at Lochenkit and on 13 April 1685 sat on a justiciary commission at Wigtown which sentenced three women, Margaret Maclauchlan and two sisters Margaret and Agnes Wilson, to death, who, on appearance with one Margaret Maxwell on charges of conventicling, refused to join the latter in accepting the oath of abjuration. The sentence of death by drowning was consistent with the council's instructions of 13 January 1685 that commissioners should not "examine any women but such as hes been active in these courses in a signall manner, and these are to be drowned".[11] Of the three Agnes Wilson was a mere child and little difficulty appears to have been experienced by her father Gilbert in securing her release on his bond of £100, but securing a reprieve for the other two who were clearly responsible for their own actions proved more difficult. A petition was presented on behalf of the sexagenarian Margaret Maclauchlan, and Gilbert Wilson was active in Edinburgh on his eighteen-year-old daughter,

Margaret's behalf, although no petition to this effect has survived. On 30 April the council considered the matter and
thereafter issued instructions discharging the magistrates of
Edinburgh from executing the two women, and recommended
the secretaries of state to intercede with the king for a remission.
So much is fact, but what happened thereafter is uncertain.
Many words have since been written for or against martyrdom
of the two women.[12] Much has hinged on their date of supposed
execution. If they were drowned on 2 May 1685 it is con-
ceivable that the stay of execution came too late to save them,
although a determined horseman could surely have traversed
the 100 odd miles between Edinburgh and Wigtown even in
that short space of time. The case for 2 May as the date of
execution is not however strong and 11 May, the date given in
most traditional accounts of their execution, must be preferred.
According to these accounts, none of which is earlier than 1711,
the two women were tied to stakes before the advancing tide,
the elder of the two being tied to the foremost stake possibly
in the hope that her death would persuade Margaret Wilson
to take the oath and save herself. Both women, however, remained stalwart, and although efforts were apparently made
after Margaret Maclauchlan had been "held down within the
water by one of the town officers by his halbert at her throat"
to persuade Margaret Wilson to subscribe the proffered
abjuration oath,[13] she remained obdurate until she too was
thrust beneath the waves by the town's officer with his halbert.
But did the women die, or are the accounts pious accounts in-
vented for the book of martyrs? Why was the "reprieve" not
effected if eleven and not two days separated the council's
recommendation and the actual "execution"? The truth may
never be known, but it should be pointed out that the council's
recommendation was only for a stay of execution and although
intercession with the king could scarcely have been made in the
time available, other counsels may have prevailed. The mere
technicality that the magistrates of Edinburgh were named in
the recommendation, rather than the magistrates of Wigtown,
could have invalidated the whole proceedings. If, moreover,
the graphic accounts of the women's deaths are late, and therefore somewhat suspect in their bias, this may only be in respect

of detail. The accounts were written in the lifetime of many who must have known the true facts and if the substance had been fictitious some rejoinder might have been expected. The weight of evidence commencing with undefined charges in 1686 in the *Informatory Vindication* by Renwick and Alexander Shields in which their persecutors are charged with "drowning women, some of a very young and some of an exceeding old age" to the more specific charge in Shield's *Short Memorial of Sufferings and Grievances* in which the women are first named, points fairly conclusively to their death.[14] The fact that they were women and the unusual nature of their death has made this the *cause célèbre* of the killing times, but it is perhaps unfortunate that their case has often obscured the real implications of the persecutions in which many other women suffered almost as grievously for their adherence to the presbyterian cause.

In this respect it is almost impossible to distinguish between Cameronians, who fully concurred with the sentiments expressed in the *Apologetical Declaration*, and presbyterians who refused to recognize the supremacy of the state in ecclesiastical matters. Such fine distinctions do not appear to have troubled the conscience of many of the commissioners, and an act of parliament of 8 May 1685 condemning to death preachers and hearers at conventicles confirmed their interpretation that recusants might be similarly treated. During that month the summary executions proceeded apace, spurred on by declarations in the parliament which met on 23 April that it should legislate apace to destroy "that desperat phanaticall and irreclamable partie who have brought us to the brink of ruine and dissgrace".[13] In even more vituperative mood, the new Chancellor, Perth, declared "we have a new sect sprung up among us from the dunghill, the very dreggs of the people who kill by pretended inspiration . . . whose idoll is that accursed paper the Covenant".[16]

If such fears of the power of the Remnant were totally unjustified, they were spurred by the fear that the imminent invasion by the forfeited Earl of Argyll would be the occasion of another general rising. Argyll's only hope for the success of his expedition which sailed from Holland on 2 May lay in a general presbyterian rising, but in this he was to be sadly disappointed. Repression had effectively done its work among presbyterians in general, and the Cameronians in particular refused to join a rebellion which included within its ranks those who had been untrue to the covenants. The two forces ranged against James VII were obliged to go their separate ways, and while unity would probably have achieved little, the attitude of the Cameronians to the Argyll rising is indicative of their isolation from political and ecclesiastical realities. Argyll himself was equally unrealistic in his venture and although his standard bore the motto: "For God and Religion against Poperie, Tyrannie, Arbitrary Government, and Errestianisme",[17] few of the many in Scotland who would have readily concurred in such principles were prepared to join him. In the face of superior government forces his supporters melted away, leaving a solitary Argyll, apprehended as he crossed the Cart on 18 June, to face ignominious execution twelve days later.

With one rebellion curbed the administration was free to resume its battle against the Cameronians who, at the height of the Argyll alarm, had chosen on 28 May to reassert their own principles in a declaration affixed to the cross at Sanquhar, Dumfriesshire. This manifesto issued on behalf of "the contending and suffering remnant of the true presbyterians of the Church of Scotland" homologated previous declarations and ended with an appeal to comfort "a poor wasted, wronged, wounded, reproached, despised and bleeding remnant".[18] The council's reply was predictable; their efforts against this further challenge to their authority was to redouble their moves to apprehend Renwick and his associates. Their attempts produced several other victims during the remainder of the year, but, as the ostensible solidarity of the established church increased through the successful harrying of presbyterians into its fold, the necessity to pursue the few remaining Cameronians became less urgent. As a result the number of persecutions dramatically diminished in 1686, and only one Cameronian, David Steel of Nether Skellyhill near Lesmahagow, was executed during the course of the year. Non-conformity at last appeared to have submitted and with the death of Alexander

E

Peden, the last of the presbyterian field preachers, who met a natural death and so eluded his enemies to the end, a united church seemed for the first time since the Restoration to be an attainable achievement.

This was not to be owed less to the few remaining Cameronians than to the folly of James VII who in his moment of triumph turned to a new policy designed to aid his coreligionists. Converts to catholicism such as the Earl of Perth who was chancellor, and his brother Lord Melfort, a secretary of state, were joined by the Earl of Moray who became commissioner in 1686 and announced his conversion in the following year. Nevertheless, and in spite of an offer of trade concessions between England and Scotland, James was baulked in his attempt to persuade parliament to pass legislation in 1686 for the relief of catholics, being informed by the Estates that they would "goe as great lengths therein as our conscience will allow".[19] Subsequent events demonstrated that the conscience of the majority on this issue was rigidly opposed to the proposed concessions. The removal of opponents such as the treasurer, Queensberry, the Lord Advocate, Sir George MacKenzie and Bishop Bruce of Dunkeld produced no marked advantage to the king's cause and the opposition led by the Duke of Hamilton and Sir George Lockhart succeeded in defeating every proposal for catholic relief. To effect this, James was forced to have recourse to a Privy Council edict of 14 September which granted to catholics "the free private exercise of their religion in houses".[20] At the same time he pressed ahead with his own scheme for converting the abbey church of Holyrood into a catholic Chapel Royal and the establishment by Jesuits there of a school and printing press.

In the following year, which opened with the dismissal of Archbishop Cairncross of Glasgow for allowing an anti-catholic sermon to go unpunished, James pressed on with more extensive schemes for toleration. In February 1687 an Indulgence was issued which if it stopped short of a general Indulgence was nevertheless generous in its terms, if also demonstrating the king's true proclivity in so far as catholics and quakers were favoured at the expense of presbyterian dissenters. The only restrictions placed upon the former was that they should not worship in the fields, that they should not make public processions in the high streets of royal burghs and that they should not invade protestant churches by force. Otherwise they were to be allowed to worship in private houses or chapels in the case of catholics and in "any place or places appointed for their worship" in the case of quakers.[21] Presbyterians were not so generously served; they were to meet only in private houses for the purpose of hearing ministers who must themselves have accepted the Indulgence, and they were specifically forbidden "to build meeting-houses, or to use outhouses or barns".[22] Field conventicles were to be punished according to the utmost severity of the law. If few remained to cavil at this last restriction many presbyterians still found these concessions inhibiting, and insistence upon an oath of non-resistance was equally invidious to the scruples of many.

This reluctance coupled with a desire to extend further privileges to his co-religionists probably prompted the issue of a second Indulgence in June 1687. In this all restrictions, with the exception of those against field conventicles, were lifted and leave was granted to all subjects "to meet and serve God after their own way, be it in private houses, chapels, or places purposely hired or built for that use".[23] The effect was immediate. Ministers and others who were released from prison were joined by exiled ministers from Holland. Many of these met in Edinburgh on 20 July and on the following day penned an address of thanks to the king. At the same time plans were drawn up for the implementation of the Indulgence and the setting up of an embryonic presbyterian structure. The bitter in-fighting which had characterized the reception of the earlier Indulgences had all but disappeared and co-operation was now the key-note. Presbyteries were to be established and meetings of these courts were to be convened at least once per month at which ministers were to seek the advice and submit themselves to the discipline of their brother ministers. The setting up of meeting houses was also to be a co-operative venture since it was conceded that "it cannot be expected, that there can be as many meeting-houses as parishes".[24] Provision was also made for encouraging students, licensing them and ordaining them to congregations. In practice the presbyterians set about re-erecting the body of their church, in so far as this could be accomplished within the terms of the privileges conceded to them.

To Renwick and his followers alone these concessions were unacceptable. A *Testimony against the Toleration* was transmitted to a meeting of ministers in January 1688. The tradition of field conventicling was maintained by Renwick and his followers who even ventured to hold such gatherings in the vicinity of Edinburgh. It was after one such meeting that Renwick, who had ventured into the capital, was recognized and captured after a chase through the streets on 1 February. After examination by the council he was declared an irreconcilable opponent of the king. This position was maintained at his trial seven days later and made sentence of death inevitable. Thereafter, intensive efforts were made even by his prosecutors to gain some acknowledgment of the king's authority which might be used to mitigate the sentence. It was all to no avail, but these efforts in themselves are clearly indicative of the changing ecclesiastical climate. The shadow of a religious rebellion had been dispelled by the Indulgences and the good sense of the presbyterian ministers, who were even willing to pray for a catholic king in order to retain their privileges. In isolation the Cameronians were increasingly revealed as a small and insignificant sect who despite their spirited and sonorous declarations had not possessed the power since 1679 of initiating, far less sustaining, war against the state. After Renwick's death only a few sparks of their old spirit remained as exemplified in the rescue about 20 June 1688 of one of Renwick's companions, David Houston, who had been apprehended in Ireland and was being sent to Edinburgh. In the military sweep which followed, the summary execution in July of a boy of sixteen, George Wood, finally brought the killing times to an end.

In terms of human life the final toll exacted during this period was not great, some 78 victims having been summarily despatched in the fields either for refusing the oath of abjuration, attempting to resist or escape capture. To these must be added those who paid the ultimate penalty after normal judicial proceedings, but the final total does not greatly exceed

100 in all. The exact number is perhaps unimportant. Accredited martyrs are sufficiently numerous to engage their supporters and their detractors. Such irrelevancies, coupled with the age-long debate as to whether the victims should be regarded as traitors, fanatics or martyrs, have obscured the real implications of persecutions whose ultimate design through wholesale fining, imprisonment and banishment was part of a systematic campaign aimed at harrying all presbyterians into conformity with the established church. It is in terms of that campaign, paradoxically foiled by declarations of Indulgence designed to help catholics, rather in terms of those who courted martyrdom by denying the authority of the crown, that the era of the killing times deserves its place in the history of religious and political intolerance.

Chapter Nine

THE TRIUMPH OF PRESBYTERIANISM

As THE INDULGENCE of June 1687 became operative the extent to which coercion had achieved its end was finally revealed. In at least six southern counties—Ayr, Dumfries, Kirkcudbright, Lanark, Renfrew and Wigtown—the vast majority of parishioners withdrew from their parish churches. If the curate of Kirkinner who saw his congregation dwindle to one, the laird of Baldoon, before he too left was exceptional, the number of worshippers in other parishes was but a tiny minority of the total communicant roll. Elsewhere the situation was much more fluid. Very few presbyterian meeting houses —three or four is one estimate—were erected north of the Tay and these were "very little frequented or encouraged".[1] South of that line the situation was much more mixed and in the south-east several parishes followed the example of Carrington where the deposed minister returned and quickly drew his old parishioners to the new meeting house. The return of their old minister, James Kirkpatrick, in November 1687 "to visit the said parochiners and to preach unto them . . . quhilk time he has continued the ministeriall functions among them except four or five",[2] was characteristic, although by no means universal, of many parishes in the east and south-east, especially those in which the minister had been previously deprived or a strong conventicling tradition established. On the other hand for many schism was unacceptable and for this reason, if for no other, the episcopal church may have survived had it not been for the increasingly overt catholicism of the king. Nevertheless, in spite of seething discontent, there is little indication that the Scots were inclined to rise on this score. The events which swept James VII from his throne were initiated in England in which a similar policy had aroused a strong opposition who were willing to act in defence of their liberties. At their invitation William of Orange arrived at Torbay in

November 1688, and a month later James fled to France—the Glorious Revolution had been effected.

The Revolution carried through in England was to have far-reaching effects in Scotland. But this was not immediately evident, and, with the exception of the south-west where the rabbling of the curates took place and in the capital itself where the mob wrecked the Chapel Royal and drove out the Jesuits, no far-reaching changes at first took place. The rabblings in which many of the established clergy found themselves ejected from their kirks and manses and forced in many cases to suffer the personal indignity of having their vestments cut off and burned may have been predictable in areas in which persecution had been unduly severe. But they also demonstrated that intolerance was not the prerogative of the erstwhile opponents of presbyterianism. If, moreover, the assumption underlying such actions was that their cause had at length triumphed over that of the established episcopal church that hope was still somewhat short of realization. Even the acceptance of William and Mary as joint sovereigns by the Convention of the Estates in April 1689 did not make such a change inevitable, although it is clear that such changes were being contemplated. In particular, the assertive clause of the Claim of Right: "That Prelacy and the superiority of any office in the Church above Presbyters, is, and hath been a great and insupportable grievance and trouble to this Nation, and contrary to the inclinations of the generality of the people, ever since the Reformation (they having been reformed from Popery by Presbyters), and therefore ought to be abolished",[3] indicated in which direction events were moving, and may indeed have been inserted in an attempt to commit William to the overthrow of episcopacy. Two days later the point was driven home by a condemnation in the Articles of Grievances of the Act of Supremacy of 1669 on the grounds that it was "inconsistent with the establishment of the church government now desyred".[4]

Although presbyterian pressure was increasingly brought to bear upon William as a means of reinforcing claims made to him in Holland that "if Scotland was left to free choice, of three parts two would be presbyterian",[5] it was by no means certain that William would be bound by his acceptance of the Claim of Right. Supporters of the moderate episcopal settlement were numerous and may indeed have been in the majority. Moreover, William quickly realized the value of bishops to the crown both as a means of controlling the church and administering the state. In the circumstances the maintenance of episcopacy was a possibility not to be denied. Much, however, depended upon the attitude of the church itself.

The church confronted by the effects of toleration and the threat of catholicism had not been unmindful of its position. In December 1688 the bishops had appointed the bishops of Edinburgh and Orkney to proceed to London to safeguard their interests. In the event, only Rose, Bishop of Edinburgh, made the journey south where he found on his arrival in the capital that James had fled and William was soundly entrenched. Rose could get little advice from the English bishops while a request to the king that he should receive a deputation of Scots episcopal nobility and gentry was rejected "lest he might give jealousy and umbrage to the presbyterians".[6] On the other hand he would not permit the presbyterians to come to him in numbers, and he would not, he stated, "allow above two of either party at a time to speak to him in church matters".[7] The king did, however, inform Rose through the medium of Compton, Bishop of London, that:

> He now knows the state of Scotland much better than he did when he was in Holland, for, while there, he was made believe that Scotland generally all over was Presbyterian, but now sees the great body of the nobility and gentry are for Episcopacy, and 'tis the trading and inferior sort are for Presbytery; wherefore he now bids me tell you that, if you will undertake to serve him to the purpose that he is served here in England, he will take you by the hand, support the Church and Order, and throw off the Presbyterians.[8]

To this Rose replied that he had no instructions to act for the Scottish church in the crisis. While this was so, Rose, in an interview with William on the following day, went far to seal the fate of the episcopal church when, in answer to the prince's comment that he hoped affairs in Scotland would follow the example of England, he replied: "Sir, I will serve you so far as law, reason, or conscience shall allow me".[9]

In taking this attitude Rose was only foreshadowing the attitude adopted by the Scottish bishops in general. Many ministers followed their lead and although a proclamation of 13 April 1689 ordering public prayers for the new king and queen brought few deprivations, yet another of 6 August, which invited members of congregations to denounce defaulters to the council, brought the number of deprivations by 7 November to 182. Faced with this uncompromising Jacobitism William had little choice but to abolish episcopal government in the church. But nothing was done at this juncture to authorize presbyterian government in its stead and not until confronted by a parliamentary refusal to grant supply did William finally signify his approval to an act establishing presbyterian government in the church.

This legislation of 7 June 1690 appeared to fulfil the presbyterian demands. The conciliar system of church government previously established in 1592 was now to be fully revived and in particular General Assemblies were to meet again. In addition patronage was abolished, the Act of Supremacy repealed and ministers ousted in 1662 were to be restored to their former parishes. Nevertheless, victory was by no means total. Patronage had been abolished, but popular election by parishioners was not to be allowed, the right of a congregation being limited to approving or disapproving of the nominee put forward by the heritors and elders. More significantly the church had not entirely freed itself from state control, and assemblies, while now allowed to meet, were still to be subject to the wishes of the crown and parliament. In this respect the realization of the Melvillian doctrine of the two kingdoms which would have given the church total independence of the state in its own sphere of responsibility had not been achieved. The covenants were equally no nearer acceptance although this perhaps mattered little to all but the Cameronians, who predictably refused to accept this settlement and remained outside the new establishment.

The extent to which the country as a whole favoured the

restoration of presbyterianism is a matter of doubt. Shortage of presbyterian ministers gave the appearance in certain areas of strong episcopal continuation and the influence of the aristocracy undoubtedly veered in that direction. Again, while it is true that only a minority of the populace took advantage of the Indulgences of 1687, it does not necessarily follow that those who preferred thereafter to remain within the fold of the newly-established church were pro-episcopal in their sympathies. Adherence to the established church was an accepted principle in itself and would prevail irrespective of the nature of the organization. In certain areas this attitude was made all the easier as presbyteries during the Restoration period had been allowed a great deal of latitude by individual bishops, while throughout Scotland the fact that doctrine remained unaltered by organizational change inevitably eased the transition to presbyterianism. For these reasons while it may be accepted that a majority of the populace was committed to the established episcopal church before the Revolution it may be equally true that when in turn presbyterianism came to represent the national conscience it too could fairly claim to represent the majority viewpoint.

An overall assessment of this nature is, however, meaningless in an era which set little store by majority views. In terms of geographical distribution throughout the country, a more significant pattern emerges. The west and south-west in which the Indulgence had claimed a large number of adherents displayed overwhelming support for the new establishment. If the east and south-east could not entirely match this zeal certain areas such as the Merse and Tweeddale made a brave attempt to do so and, although pockets of episcopal support are evident throughout the Lothians in general, the area seems to have possessed a fairly sizeable presbyterian majority. North of the Forth, Fife, Stirling and southern Perthshire were staunchly presbyterian, but northern Perthshire was not. In general, the area north of the Tay, and in particular the north-eastern counties of Aberdeen, Moray and Banff, showed a strong proclivity for episcopacy. But even there presbyterian sympathizers were not entirely lacking. This area also possessed a strong leavening of catholics, and episcopal solidarity in this region was certainly less comprehensive than that exhibited for presbyterianism in the south-west. Nevertheless, it may be generally accepted that north of the Tay the majority of the populace were pro-episcopal, while south of that line the opposite was true.

Not unnaturally the majority of ministers were in favour of the episcopal establishment in which they had been nurtured. As a result the General Assembly which met in 1690 was composed of only some 180 ministers and elders none of whom was drawn from the area north of the Tay. Small though this body was, and certainly unrepresentative of the ministry of the church, it pressed ahead with its plans for the implementation of a presbyterian programme for which it believed, and probably rightly believed, that it had the general support of the people at large. Many more ministers were dispossessed and little evidence of compromise was evident. All ministers, probationers and elders were required to subscribe to the Westminster Confession. Private communion and baptism were forbidden and commissions were appointed to proceed against recalcitrant clergy, many of whom were deposed on the slightest grounds. This policy was all the more remarkable as the presbyterians did not have the ministers adequately to staff their new establishment. Nevertheless, the Assembly of 1691 was no more willing to compromise, and the rejection of William's plea for moderation resulted in the king adjourning the Assembly which did not meet again until January 1692, when further defiance of William by its refusal to admit episcopal clergy to sign a formula of his own devising caused another dissolution.

A direct confrontation between church and state seemed once again possible and this likelihood grew as the intolerance demonstrated by the victorious presbyterians increased. The campaign against recalcitrant episcopal clergy gained momentum in 1694. In that year the Assembly, meeting for the first time since 1692, endorsed an act of parliament of the previous year which had decreed that no person could be a minister of the established church unless he had taken the oath accepting William as *de facto* king, had subscribed to the Westminster Confession and had accepted presbyterianism as the only form

of church government. By virtue of this enactment a number of
northern clergy, who had challenged the validity of it, were
deposed and at the same time the cathedral of Aberdeen was
seized. A head-on collision between king and Assembly seemed
unavoidable as the latter continued to ignore the wishes of the
crown. But for the wise counsel of William Carstares, William's
chief adviser on Scottish affairs, who had himself suffered
torture and imprisonment in 1684, the assembly of 1695 might
never have met. A total breach was narrowly avoided and the
Assembly reluctantly accepted a compromise which, while
forbidding deposed episcopal ministers to celebrate baptisms
or marriages, withdrew the requirement that they accept
presbyterianism and furthermore offered an indulgence to
those taking the oath of allegiance within a certain specified
time. More than 100 accepted this offer and the resolution of
this problem went some way towards securing a better relationship between the crown and the church. In the same year
compromise was also reached over the question of summoning
General Assemblies. Difficulties had arisen in 1692 and 1694
when it was clear that the king intended to utilize his prerogative right on questions affecting the meetings of the Assembly.
The church took the viewpoint that this right was in their
keeping alone, but eventually did not proceed with their
claims on the king's assurance through his commissioner that
the assembly would be summoned annually at a suitable time
and place. The passing of the "Barrier Act" in 1697 added a
final touch to the settlement of the constitution of the newly-
established Church of Scotland. This ensured by laying down
the method by which legislation was to be passed through the
General Assembly that hasty or unpopular acts could not be
rushed through an assembly by any prevailing faction. All
desired legislation was to be initially proposed to the assembly
as an "overture" and, if approved, was to be sent to presbyteries for their consideration. If supported by a majority of
presbyteries the measure would then be brought before the
assembly for final approval.

   With these measures the newly-established church seemed
fairly satisfied. Nevertheless, the latent struggle between church
and state was not entirely dead. In 1698 the assembly declined

to accept the view that the church was founded on the inclinations of the people and acts of parliament. Instead its
commission asserted: "We do believe and own that Jesus
Christ is the only Head and King of this Church".[10] Anti-
Erastianism was never far from the surface and was to re-
emerge as a powerful and often destructive force within the
church of the eighteenth and nineteenth centuries. But in the
meantime opposition to the state tended to concentrate on
opposing all attempts at toleration. Active persecution would
actually have been preferred and as a result the Scottish
bishops and non-juring clergy who continued their ministra-
tions, but refused the oath of allegiance, suffered considerable
hardships. Queen Anne, after her accession in 1702, was well
disposed to their appeal for help, but opinion in Scotland was
far from favourable. An assembly of 1703 went as far as to
inform the queen that presbytery was agreeable to the Word
of God and the only government of Christ's Church in the
Kingdom, while the introduction of a bill into parliament in
1703 which would have allowed for the toleration of all non-
Roman dissenters had to be dropped when a commission of
the assembly presented a remonstrance against "any legal
toleration to those of prelatical principles".[11]

In the reign of Anne the presbyterians were much on the
defensive. Toleration was a minor fear in comparison to that
posed by a possible Jacobite restoration. If the union of 1707
gained their reluctant support because of that fear, this was
compounded thereafter by fears of threats from a British
parliament with a permanent anglican majority. Three acts
of 1712 seemed to justify that anxiety. The first of these, the
Yule Vacance Act, which reversed the abolition in 1690 of
the Christmas vacation in the law courts was vexatious but not
over-important. Much more serious implications arose over
the Toleration Act and the Patronage Act. The Toleration Act
was directly inspired by the case of James Greenshields, an
episcopal minister who had come from Ireland and had held
services in Edinburgh in 1709 using the anglican prayer-book.
As far as the authorities were concerned Greenshields, who had
taken the oath of allegiance, had nevertheless no right to
minister and, on his defiance of the local presbytery, the

magistrates imprisoned him for his contumacy. An appeal to
the Court of Session had no success but in March 1711 the
House of Lords sustained his appeal and found the magistrates
liable for his costs. Greenshields was not alone in his difficulties,
however, and an equally fierce denunciation was made by the
church on all who used the liturgy of the episcopal church.
The users of the prayer book were by no means all Scots as the
English officials who came north in steadily increasing numbers
after the Union were to be followed by English clergymen who
used their own service books. English regiments likewise had
their own chaplains and followed their accustomed ways. Such
support, moreover, emboldened existing episcopal clergy who
continued to use the anglican prayer book in their meeting
houses which were constructed following the occupation of the
established parish churches by the presbyterians.

Greenshield's case brought the difficulties of such groups to
the fore, and in spite of the endeavours of presbyterian emis-
saries the Toleration Act was passed. All those of the episcopal
communion in Scotland were thenceforward to be entitled to
use the liturgy of the Church of England in their congregations
while episcopal clergymen for the future were to be permitted,
by the repeal of the 1695 act, to officiate at baptisms and
marriages. Episcopalian worship was now to be permitted in
Scotland, but with one proviso—an oath of allegiance to the
reigning monarch, who must belong to the Church of England,
and an oath abjuring the Stuart succession must be taken before
toleration could be enjoyed. Many episcopal clergy welcomed
the act, but the oath of abjuration perpetuated for the rest of
the century the schism between jurors and non-jurors. The
presbyterians were more unanimous in their condemnation of
the act, not only because of toleration, but also because the
necessity to take the oaths was extended to themselves. Few, if
any, objected to an abjuration of the Stuarts, but an oath
recognizing the sovereign as a member of the Church of
England was another matter. A schism between non-jurors and
jurors in the established church was only narrowly prevented,
but unity could not be so readily preserved on the third
measure enacted in 1712.

Patronage in the church had only been abolished in 1690

when the right of individual patrons to present ministers for institution had been abrogated in favour of heritors and elders. Now individual rights were restored, possibly in an effort to win the patrons over to the established church but also with the hope that a better qualified ministry would ensue. Such hopes, if they did exist, were not in the main to be realized, or if they did come about, were not to be the result of this act. Instead the existence of patronage continued to be a source of dissidence around which all grievances, real and imaginary, could gather. During the eighteenth and nineteenth centuries patronage was the excuse rather than the underlying reason for secession. The real issues lay much deeper, and in this respect the established church never overcame the dilemma of the covenanting era. If the responsibilities of church and state could not be evenly divided which of these two forces should be dominant?

These developments must have convinced the Cameronian remnant that they had acted wisely in refusing to comply with the uncovenanted and Erastian establishment of the presbyterian Church of Scotland in 1690. The first general meeting of this party after the Revolution was held at Douglas on 3 January 1689. About 300 armed men were present at this meeting at which it was resolved to improve the military organization of the Societies. Captains and lieutenants of companies were to effect proposals to this effect. The motivation for this military activity was, however, changing from that of self-defence at conventicles to a general defence of presbyterianism at large. To this end, after a meeting at Crawfordjohn on 13 February 1689, an armed retinue was despatched to Edinburgh to protect the Convention of Estates from threatened Jacobite attack. Not all of the Society People approved of this "sinful association"[12] with presbyterian malignants and a proposal to carry this activity one stage further by the formation of a regiment met bitter opposition at the general meeting held in Douglas church on 29 April 1689. After a long and heated debate, a minority agreed to support the proposal and serve in a regiment that became known as the Cameronians, and whose avowed purpose was to "resist Popery and Prelacy, and arbitrary power; and to recover and establish the work of

Reformation in Scotland".[13] Too late in their arrival to fight
at Killiecrankie where the Jacobites won the day but lost their
leader John Graham of Claverhouse, Viscount Dundee, the
Cameronians made their amends by their gallant defence of
Dunkeld on 17–18 August 1689.

This action, which turned the tide against the Jacobites,
secured the protestant revolution in Scotland, but in no way
lessened the ecclesiastical problem of the Societies. These
problems were intensified by the establishment of presbyterianism on 7 June 1690 as many adherents thereafter professed a preference for the Church of Scotland. At another
general meeting of the Societies at Douglas on 3 December 1690
their three remaining ministers—Lining, Shields and Boyd—
informed the gathering that they had joined the established
church at the November General Assembly and advised the
rest to do likewise. This suggestion met with a mixed reception,
but it was eventually determined by the majority that a declaration should be prepared which might be given by any member
to the minister of the congregation he wished to join. This was
to the effect that uniting with the establishment was not to be
considered as a "condemning of, or receding from, our former
testimony".[14] On this basis many appear to have followed the
example of their ministers and returned to the presbyterian
fold leaving the Societies numerically weak and with little
cohesion.

Without ministers and a clear sense of purpose the Societies
might have gradually withered away, but there were some
within their ranks who were determined to maintain the cove-
ants and their claims to be the "True Church of Scotland".[15]
Among these was Robert Hamilton, who had led the conventicling army at Bothwell Bridge, and had subsequently
taken refuge in Holland from which he returned in 1688. His
radical views on church-state relations which had been manifest in 1679 had in no way diminished in exile and after his
return he set about instilling new heart into Society People.
His efforts similarly inspired others and a paper prepared by
the Society, at Tinwald in Dumfriesshire, brought such a ready
response from other groups that they decided to proceed with
plans for the re-organization of the Societies. Needless to say

this was not achieved without further dissension and defection. The desire expressed in the original paper that all adherents who had heard the curates, helped the indulged or listened to the three former ministers since their entry into the Church of Scotland should be banned from the Societies was naturally not acceptable to those who failed to meet these conditions. In consequence when the Societies held another general meeting in August 1692 its principal business appears to have consisted of purging from its ranks those who "had made defection to the contrary party".[16] Thereafter their own unequivocal position was proclaimed in a declaration affixed to the cross of Sanquhar on 10 August 1692.

The Societies remained in being but at a price, for in the years which followed schism within their ranks became increasingly commonplace. This tradition was not new, for as early as 15 June 1682, James Russell, one of the murderers of Sharp, had demanded at the meeting of the Societies at Tala Linn that members should refuse to pay cess at ports or bridges and having failed to convince the majority had seceded with a few companions. The Russellites maintained this exclusiveness after the Revolution shortly after which they were to be joined by other schismatic groups each claiming divine truth for its own adherents. After the Sanquhar declaration of 1695 the Correspondences of Eskdale and Forrest seceded from the Societies and about the same period two brothers John and Andrew Harley also withdrew and formed a small sect known as the Harlites or "Cote Moor Folk", as they were sometimes called. The divisions continued apace in the eighteenth century and at least eight identifiable parties, other than the Correspondences of Eskdale and Forrest who had returned to the fold about 1709, were to be found by 1725. Two of these were the Russellites and Harlites, but the others bore such names as Adamites, Hebronites and Howdenites after their respective leaders, others were led by Peter Grant and William Wilson respectively and yet another group appears to have been organized by ministers in Nithsdale. Some of these such as the latter and the followers of John Hepburn—the Hebronites—were closer to the established church than the main body of the Societies, who in 1706 found an acceptable preacher in

John McMillan and thereafter are referred to as McMillanites, but others such as the Russellites and Howdenites were much more radical and even fanatical in their adherence to the covenant. Few of these sects outlived their founders by many years and when in turn the established church became schismatic, many of the disaffected found refuge in a secession church. The McMillanites, however, retained their fervour and emerged in 1743 as the Reformed Presbyterian Church which if no longer interested in converting other people to their views continues to perpetuate to this day the ideas of the covenant for which their forebears had suffered.

If after their initial proclamation the ideals of the covenant became decreasingly attractive to the Scottish people, and in the long run appear to represent intolerance, it is perhaps ironic that the high ideals which characterized the National Covenant of 1638 should be eventually perpetuated only in the tenets of a small and insignificant sect. This has frequently, and with some justification, been attributed to the excesses which characterized the Solemn League and Covenant of 1643. That agreement certainly caused deep division in the covenanting movement, and it is doubtful whether at any point the majority of Scots would have concurred in the idea of a general presbyterian crusade. On the other hand it is equally clear that the vast majority of Scots at the Restoration of 1660 expected that the presbyterian establishment would be maintained. Political expediency dictated otherwise. If the Covenanters of the Restoration period can be adjudged guilty of intolerance, it is equally true that autocracy dictated a religious settlement to which the great majority of the Scottish people were opposed. To sacrifice the covenants was one thing, to admit to state control of the church was quite another. In this respect the covenanting movement has been misjudged. For a minority the struggle against the state may have been for a full implementation of the covenant in England, Ireland and Scotland, but for most it was a purely internal struggle against state control of the church. Such a struggle had been intermittently waged since the Reformation and anti-Erastianism had become one of the most sacred beliefs of the Scottish church. To some, however, this belief had become an absolute and hence the unbending attitude of the most radical of covenanters—the Cameronians. To others, however, compromise was always possible and it was to such a solution that the indulged, and eventually the Church of Scotland, gave their blessing. In the battle towards this end the gulf which separated die-hard Covenanters and the most moderate of presbyterians was never so great as may have been imagined. In their attitude to the state control of the church Cameronian and presbyterian were agreed in principle but deeply divided in action. In the last resort the Cameronian was prepared to wage war against the state and die for his beliefs, whereas the more moderate presbyterian, who was not asked to die if he acknowledged the authority of the king, was prepared to suffer deprivation of liberty and other monetary and material penalties. If this element of compromise was reprehensible to some, such attitudes eventually won the day for the presbyterian church. An incalculable debt was nevertheless owed to the more extreme groups who ensured by their sheer determination that state interference in the affairs of the church would be minimal. The maintenance of this principle, and not the extension of presbyterianism furth of Scotland, was the real issue behind the later covenanting struggle, and every presbyterian whether he be moderate Conventicler or extreme Covenanter would have agreed that the realization of this ideal was paramount. If this principle was only partially attained in the presbyterian settlement of 1690, the ideal was never to entirely vanish. The secessions of the eighteenth and nineteenth centuries were but an extension of this problem, and if no one asked the participants to lay down their lives feeling ran equally high. In this respect the history of the Covenanters is not entirely one of religious bigotry but rather part of a more general struggle by the church against the intolerance of the state.

Chapter Ten

POST-RESTORATION SCOTLAND

THE HISTORY OF bigotry and religious intolerance which characterizes the history of late seventeenth-century Scotland is not a pleasant one. It led at least one Scottish historian to call the period "the most pitiful chapter in our annals",[1] and this judgment has been generally followed. But the justness of this verdict is open to question. The life of the nation was diversifying in many respects and the predominance accorded to political and religious matters was slowly but surely waning.

The change was most clearly evident in economic affairs. The Restoration quickened the growing interest in trade and industry which had characterized the dying years of the Cromwellian administration. In the face of opposition from England, which immediately re-introduced the machinery of mercantilism between the two countries, the Scottish parliament and Privy Council inaugurated a commercial policy designed to combat the country's economic ailments. The chief impediments to the institution of new manufactures were shortage of capital and labour, and, in order to devise a remedy, the first parliament of Charles II appointed in 1661 a committee for trade and complaints who were given power "to meet advise and prepare such overtures and acts as they shall think fit to be passed for advancing of trade, navigation and manufactories, and for that end to call for the advice and help of understanding merchants, or any who can give best information in those affairs".[2] In the same year the spirit of commercial enterprise was also expressed in an "Act Establishing Companies and Societies",[3] in which as an inducement to co-operation facilities were given to individuals to incorporate themselves into companies. This act conferred a privilege which was uncommon in England where an act of incorporation involved much trouble and personal expense. Two further acts were passed in 1661 in an endeavour to solve the problems of insufficient labour and capital. In an effort to establish a system of elementary technical operation it was enacted that "ther be in each paroche one or more persones provided and appointed upon the charges and expenses of the heritors thereof for instructing of the poore children, vagabounds and other idlers to fine and mix wooll, spin worstead and knit stockings".[4] In order to attract capital, a further enactment promised naturalization to foreigners willing to establish industries in Scotland. Neither of these acts had any discernible effects, nor had many of the others which followed in their wake. But they serve to show that a genuine desire for economic progress was evident at this time, and several companies were in fact founded on the basis of this legislation. Additional privileges were conferred upon such companies during the two decades which followed the initial enactments, but in 1681 it was deemed that sufficient progress had still not been made and early that year a conference of Scottish merchants was summoned "to give their advyse anent the causes of the decay of trade and what they should propose for the remeid thereof".[5]

As a result of the deliberations between merchants and the newly-appointed committee of trade, a more thorough protective system was evolved by council and parliament. A "mature and digested proclamation, for regulation of the manufacture and trade of the kingdom" was issued and its measures were strengthened by an "act for encouraging Trade and Manufactures".[6] By this act certain luxury goods were not to be imported, and in order to encourage home manufacturers even cambric and linen were not to be brought into the country. In addition, raw materials for certain basic industries were to be imported free of duty, and as a further incentive invested capital was not to be taxable. In view of these regulations the cost of production should have been low, as raw material was in theory made cheaper by these measures. In fact, retaliation by other countries resulted in fewer markets being available for Scottish goods and there was still great difficulty in securing adequate capital and skilled workmen. In short, this spate of legislation did not bear the fruits which might have been expected. The policy of protection might have been sound if sufficient resources had been available within Scotland, but they were not. That this was the case was certainly not the intention of parliament and the Privy Council who had superseded the Convention of Royal burghs as the primary regulators of trade and industry. Industry was escaping from municipal control, and as trade developed the staple policy which had been controlled by the burghs collapsed. The burghs were represented on committees of trade, but no longer had control in their own hands. This tendency was resisted by the convention as an infringement of trade regulations, but trade and industry quickly freed themselves of their claims. This was all the more easily accomplished in so far as the functions of the new committees often encroached upon those of the convention. Their authority was further corroded by an act of 1672. Burghs of regality and barony were given a share in the privileges of the royal burghs which thereby lost their exclusive right to overseas trade. Even when the convention attempted to promote trade, little seems to have been effected. A declaration in 1660 that it would be advantageous to "the increase of tread and the common weall of the estait of burroues within the whol Kingdome that the Fishing tread be erected within the samyn" led to no positive steps in this direction and it was as a direct result of their lack of support that the Royal Fishing Company of Scotland failed in 1670.[7] The waning influence of the convention was a healthy sign that restrictive policies were being abandoned for more positive measures to encourage trade and industry; economic activity was no longer confined to the royal burghs and unfree burghs were increasing their rights with, and sometimes without, official sanction.

The practical results of such policies were not spectacular, but were sufficiently successful to justify the attention lavished upon such schemes at a time when it might seem that religious and political issues were excluding all other issues. Indeed in some respects the period after Bothwell Bridge, including that of the "killing times", was to see more intense economic activity than that experienced in the twenty years following the Restoration. This was true in particular of the textile industry in which only modest success was achieved in consequence of the legislation of 1661 but which experienced much more rapid expansion following the trade enactment of 1681. The earlier phase, nevertheless, saw the establishment of a wool-card manufactory at Leith in 1663. Up till then all wool-cards had been imported from England and it was in an effort to rival that trade that James Currie, provost of Edinburgh, was allowed to establish the manufactory as a protected industry on condition that sufficient cards were produced for the whole country. The new price was not to exceed the old by more than ten per cent and was to revert to the original price after seven years. The council supported this enterprise not only under mercantilist theories, but to improve wool-carding by the use of new cards as imported cards had been merely re-conditioned. Such cards were, however, cheaper and smuggling posed a constant threat to this industry which nevertheless existed for many years. Similar difficulties were to face the cloth manufactories founded as a result of the 1681 act for the encouragement of trade. The best known of the joint-stock companies was that founded at Newmills near Haddington. At its establishment difficulty was experienced in finding sufficient capital and labour, but this was sufficiently sur-mounted to ensure an output of 12,000 ells of cloth per year by 1683. But in spite of the advantages conferred by various acts Scottish cloth was dearer than English and this in turn en-couraged smuggling, and even the council set a bad example by obtaining cloth from English sources. Appeals by the company to the council did, however, lead to more determined efforts to curb smuggling and, with this support, Newmills continued to receive many orders and prospered until the Revolution when renewed smuggling brought the company to an end. But Newmills is only unique in so far as its records have survived, other companies of whose affairs little is known were also established in virtue of the 1681 act. In 1683 a woollen manufactory was set up at Glasgow by James Armour for producing serges and other cloth and in the same year a broadcloth factory was instituted at Paul's Walk in Edinburgh where all the processes from the purchase of raw wool to the delivery of the finished product were performed. But success tended to be transient. Production costs were high because all high-grade wool had to be imported and the protective practices upon which the industry became increasingly dependent not only encouraged smuggling but also led to economic reprisals by other countries. The linen industry which had enjoyed modest success after the Restoration, and had employed some 12,000 workers in spinning flax, was actually retarded by retaliatory measures following upon the 1681 act. All in all the textile industry which was stimulated on one hand by favourable legislation was equally hindered by economic reprisals brought about by these self-same enactments. As a result the industry failed to live up to its early promise and went into a period of serious decline after the Revolution of 1688. Lack of success had not been for want of endeavour, however, and in other fields attempts to stimulate the economy were to pay more fruitful dividends.

Nowhere was this more evident than in Glasgow and the west of Scotland. By 1660 the city was already a thriving trading centre with tobacco already playing some small part in its rising economy. Success in trade encouraged the investment of trading profits in new industrial ventures, several of which began in the city shortly after the Restoration. Sugar refining was the most important of these industries and by 1661 had already reached sufficient dimensions that a tax of two ounces of bullion for every 60 pounds of sugar exported was exacted. Large profits appear to have resulted from this venture and other refineries were quickly established. The Wester Sugar works founded in 1667 in a single room quickly took over a whole tenement for its enterprise. Two years later the Easter Sugar works was formed on an equally prosperous basis and possessed a capital of £10,000 by 1684. One reason for its success, however, lay in a complementary rum distillery which illicitly and profitably sold its distillation in the colonies. The soap industry also flourished in the city and this received direct economic encouragement by an act of 1661 imposing an excise on each barrel of soap imported, but freeing the home producer from duty on imported raw materials. In 1667 a company known as the Glasgow Soaperie was founded to promote whale-fishing and soap boiling. The blubber was boiled at Greenock and the soap manufactured at the Soaperie.

The former process fell into other hands eventually, but soap-making thrived. Success also attended the establishment of paper-making companies. In 1675 the first paper works were founded at Dalry, on the water of Leith near Edinburgh, and by 1679 was able to produce "grey and blue paper much finer than ever this country formerly afforded".[8] Glasgow followed suit in establishing similar works and the foundations of a basic industry were quickly laid. As the city rapidly consolidated its position as Scotland's second most important burgh, its citizens' interests inevitably moved away from politics and religion to the wider horizons of trade and industry. The conventicling army which looked for support in Glasgow before the battle of Bothwell Bridge could not be expected to comprehend this change of attitude, but it undoubtedly explains the lack of enthusiasm which the citizens exhibited for their cause.

In addition to attempts to stimulate trade and industry, thoughts were also given to the development of the country's mineral wealth. In this respect optimism always ran high, although practical results were few. Promotion through example was the council's main approach to this particular problem, a grant in 1683 of a copper mine in the parish of Currie to a German, Joachim Gouel, being approved "since by working of this one mine the true method thereof might be made known to the whole nation".[9] If this particular hope was not to be realized, several lasting achievements had been recorded in other fields. But in the course of these develop-ments it had also become evident that economic reprisals would cripple progress unless new markets became available. The English colonies were ostensibly closed to the Scots and hence the growing desire that Scotland should have a colony of her own. The Scottish merchants who advocated protection realized only too well that many former markets would be barred to them and it would be essential for economic pros-perity that new markets be secured. Scots were already desir-able immigrants in some quarters and in 1670 the Governor of Jamaica urged "that all prudentiall meanes bie used to encourage ye Scottis to come hither, as being very good ser-vants".[10] Many of those who emigrated did so under com-pulsion being transported, either for their religious sympathies or as criminals or vagabonds, but voluntary emigration proved attractive to some. Scotland had no need to fear from loss of population through emigration and to this end a colony of her own was even more desirable "especiallie considering that there are many Scotts men alreadie planted . . . who, heareing of a designe of a Scott's plantatione for which they have longed these many yearis, will be glad to remove themselves and families to any place appointed, for that will be a considerable beginning to the said plantatione".[11] On the whole, Scots already settled in the American plantations were disliked by colonial governments who saw them as willing accomplices of the enterprising Scottish traders who defied the English navigation laws and operated in the North American colonies. In spite of precautions this illicit trade thrived, and the success of these ventures was often attributed to the Scots already settled in the colonies. In this respect many colonial governors would have agreed with the Governor of New Hampshire in 1682 who complained: "There are several Scot's men that inhabit here, and are great interlopers and bring in quantities of goods underhand from Scotland".[12]

The desire for an independent Scottish colony found ultimate expression in a memorandum presented to the council in 1681 and entitled *A Memorial Concerning the Scottish Plantation to be Erected in Some Place of America*. The probable location and the procedure to be adopted for its foundation are discussed and the view expressed that "the same if effectuall, may prove of great advantage to the countrey".[13] A keen insight into commercial problems is shown in this document and the same acumen characterizes a further memorial submitted to the council of trade in which foreign and inland trade, shipping and the general economic position of the country are thoroughly examined. It was this spirit which pervaded the promoters of the Company of Scotland trading to Africa and the Indies in 1695, and had some of the wisdom demonstrated in the memoranda been exhibited in practice that particular venture might have proved less disastrous.

Within the next few years two attempts were made to form Scottish settlements within the territories occupied by English colonists. Both were motivated by religious persecution and as such stand apart from the aspirations revealed in the memorandum of 1681, but serve to show that religious fervour had not quenched the spirit of enterprise. The presbyterian colony of Stuart's Town in South Carolina was essentially a place of refuge, but the emigrants who sailed to the quaker colony of East New Jersey were not entirely activated by the desire to escape persecution. This colony was founded chiefly through the efforts of the celebrated Scottish quaker, Robert Barclay of Urie, who intended it as an asylum for the persecuted, but as quakers were little troubled in Scotland the design seems to have been national rather than sectarian. Many prominent members of the Scottish administration gave assistance to the scheme and considerable emphasis was placed upon the fact that Scotsmen were among the proprietors. Examination of the announcements publicizing the scheme shows that a general appeal was made to all Scots and in consequence a high percentage of the emigrants were neither quakers, nor those fleeing from religious persecution. By 1683 Scottish emigrants were arriving in considerable numbers and this flow reached its peak in 1684, the year in which Barclay showed great enterprise and energy. The Scottish settlers soon formed an important part of the population of East New Jersey in which they quickly settled down to the task of cultivating the fertile soil. The small colony of Stuart's Town, founded in 1684 by a band of self-exiled Covenanters wishing to escape persecution, had a much unhappier existence. The scheme was initiated in 1682 in a spirit of colonizing zeal, but political and religious intrigue led to its almost immediate collapse. But a small group persisted and the settlement was effected in 1684. From the first, animosity existed between the Scots and English authorities. As a result, defence was neglected and in 1686 a Spanish force destroyed the settlement. Nevertheless, in these two enterprises, new desires and aspirations were clearly evident and if religious persecution provided the spur in both cases, economic motivation was also present and was rapidly to become foremost as religious issues became increasingly less relevant.

This is equally evident in terms of royal administration and even a crown-dominated parliament could be raised to opposition by fiscal measures. More often than not the house was guided by material interests and whereas religious issues went unheeded until James VII utilized toleration to promote catholicism, economic measures were often subject to challenge. In 1681 government measures for selling grain and relaxing the usury laws were withdrawn after opposition, and it was the rejection of an excise bill in 1686 that persuaded the Lord of the Articles to dismiss the house rather than press toleration measures to a division. Until that occasion no major issues were challenged, but debates were often lively. Opposition of this nature was at its height in 1673, but little of this was the result of genuine parliamentarianism but rather caused by a growing spirit of opposition to Lauderdale. Nevertheless, parliament was slowly assuming a new character and this too was indicative of a diversification of interest in post-Restoration Scotland.

Such diversification was however restricted to a relatively small proportion of urban society. Four-fifths of Scotland's estimated population of just over one million were still dependent on the soil for their livelihood and their lot altered little during the course of the seventeenth century. The soil over much of Scotland was poor and, if capable of growing crops at all, frequently only yielded enough to maintain a bare subsistence economy. Where it was possible to improve the yield short leases made this unprofitable, as improvement inevitably led to higher rents or eviction. But in most cases the system of "infield-outfield" husbandry, which led to the best arable land—the infield—being under constant cultivation, mitigated against any possible improvements. The division of the infield into rigs which were individually allocated meant that farms were seldom compact units and in this respect also the radical changes required for improvement could rarely come from the tenant farmers, but had to be initiated by proprietors. But few if any of these land-owners evinced any interest in so doing, and even if the will to improve had existed the capital required to effect change was seldom forthcoming in the seventeenth century. Exploitation of tenants was more often than not the sole interest of most proprietors

POST-RESTORATION SCOTLAND

in their land. Such a policy in itself could increase yield, and grain output does seem to have risen until the famine years of the last decade of the seventeenth century, but it also could lead to much bitterness between tenants and land-owners. The resultant social and economic conflict could be reflected in other ways and the social division between Conventiclers and their opponents can be viewed in many respects as such a struggle. The Conventiclers derived their support almost entirely from the peasantry and small tenant farmers while ranged against them were the land-owners and much of urban society. The ideas of the godly minority may have appealed to the underprivileged, not only in religious terms but also as a means of expressing discontent which stemmed initially from social and economic grievances.

Such grievances were far removed from the urbanity exhibited in the fields of politics, industry and trade and even more remote from the cultural life of Restoration Scotland. Nowhere was this more appositely demonstrated than in the field of law, as an era which witnessed summary executions and a ready facility to expedite the law by judicial torture and suborning of witnesses, but which also proved to be one of the most important in the development of the law itself. In this respect the most important and enduring contribution was *The Institutions of the Law of Scotland* published by Sir James Dalrymple of Stair, only two years after the battle of Bothwell Bridge. Stair, who had become Lord President of the Court of Session, but was eventually forced into exile by his opposition to the Test Act, was a man of wide experience and genius. Before his work, members of the College of Justice had to rely on the "Practicks", which were merely compilations of previous decisions arranged alphabetically under subject headings and lacked any discussion of the basic issues which underlay the law. On the other hand, the *Institutions* was more than a mere compendium of existing law: rather a philosophical and political treatise which comprehended a deduction from the original sources of Roman law and its commentators and a comparison of the law of Scotland with that of other lands. The fundamental value of Stair's work was that he stated the ultimate principle of Scots Law so clearly and it is largely owing to his labours that Scotland possesses a scientific system of law based upon the philosophical principle of starting with a right and ending with a vindication. Stair's influence in legal circles and on the survival of Scots law is incalculable, but he did not work in a vacuum. He was not an isolated genius but the apogee of a much wider movement which in terms of law found equal cogent expression in Sir George MacKenzie's *Institutions* of 1684. MacKenzie of Rosehaugh—"The Bluidy Advocate MacKenzie, who for his worldly wit and wisdom, had been to the rest as a god"[14]—has been vilified as a persecutor of Covenanters, but he has also wider claims to fame which in some measure atone for his unbending juridical severity. As a lawyer he not only practised and wrote about law, but was one of the main promoters of an Advocates' Library. Founded in 1682, the library was quickly well stocked, not only with legal texts but also with volumes of philosophy and classical literature, and on the very eve of the Revolution of 1688 MacKenzie himself gave an inaugural address extolling the merits of learning.

If such sentiments found expression in legal circles during this period, this development did not extend to the field of literature. An era of political and religious turmoil may not have been conducive to literary production although there was a considerable reissue of the works of older writers which did much to maintain the Scots vernacular tradition. Several native Scots were also writing in England and several of their plays, including Thomas Sydserf's *The Coffee House*, were produced at Holyroodhouse during the stay of the Duke of York. But one native writer was to the fore, none other than Sir George MacKenzie on whom Dryden conferred the title "That noble wit of Scotland".[15] A typical literary amateur, MacKenzie wrote all his works in the little spare time that his legal duties allowed him. His style follows that of English writers of the same period, but he does not avoid Scotticisms, and in 1660 he published *Aretina*, the earliest example of a Scottish novel. It is a voluminous tale written in exalted and "conceited" language, but displays bright and exuberant touches. But his most important work is undoubtedly *The Religious Stoic*, published in 1663 and written in the prose style of Sir

Thomas Browne. The author's personality bursts through its pages and the work is distinguished by a daintiness of classical allusion and allegorical interpretation which make it a pleasure to read. These qualities also distinguish the *Moral Essays* but they are more commonplace and less quaint. Least successful of all are MacKenzie's poems, the most important of which "Caelia's Country House and Closet" is a bad imitation of English verse in a similar genre.

In MacKenzie's works may be discerned the first faint indica-tions of the literary revival of the eighteenth century, but he stood alone and with the exception of Leighton's sermons little of literary worth was produced during the covenanting era. On the other hand, the Covenanters made a definite contribu-tion to Scottish political theory by way of their literary attacks on the royal prerogative. The anonymous *Ius Populi Vindicatum* written shortly after the Pentland Rising had to meet a situ-ation in which the civil powers, including parliament, were hostile to the covenant and therefore the appeal to the people was an appeal against parliament as well as against the king. It is argued that the primeval privilege of self-defence remains in every person, and since men would not establish a civil state unless that state was better than the natural one, it must be assumed that the ruler was chosen on trust to keep certain fundamental rights inviolate. Thus, when authority fails to maintain that trust, individuals may join together as in their natural state and resist authority in the cause of the true religion. In this respect the people are the ultimate party which truly understands and obeys the fundamental law of reason and of God. This right of resistance was a new development brought about by the course of events, and this doctrine was re-emphasized in the Cameronian Alexander Shields' *A Hind Let Loose* published in 1687. The second head or chapter of this work examines the authority of a tyrant and in it the author insists that no man may recognize tyranny as a lawful power. The idea of two distinct covenants of the king and the people with God, and the king with the people alone is re-iterated from earlier theorists, but Shields insists that if the govern-ment does not have the stamp of God's authority the people may act in order to uphold God's injunctions and goes so far as to expound the doctrine that even individuals possess the power to uphold the law against the ruler. The practical application of such doctrines at the time of the Cameronian persecutions is only too evident. Political considerations played a similar part in the refutation of such doctrines and a defence of absolutism was undertaken by Sir George MacKenzie in his *Ius Regium* published in 1684. But there is little original in this work and the principles upon which he rests the claims of monarchy are stereotyped seventeenth-century concepts. The essence of monarchy according to MacKenzie is its supreme and absolute power, but this title does not imply any more than is necessary for government and "jurisdiction not dominion" is taken to represent the proper limits of kingship.[16] Little is achieved other than a clever refutation of the Covenanters' case and they on their part were equally concerned in the practical application of their arguments. But their arguments are worthy of note in demonstrating that speculation as well as action had their place in the history of the period.

If political theory still remained rooted in the religious controversies of the age other theorists were more forward looking in their outlook. Cartography was already a prominent activity, but it was in the realm of pure science that Scots excelled and were by their achievements to rival the success of the Royal Society in England. In this respect Scotland was to produce a genius second only to Newton in the world of physics and mathematics. This was James Gregory who published in 1663 a major treatise entitled *Optica Promota* in which he gave an account of mirrors and lenses and a description of the earliest reflecting telescope. Before Gregory's discovery great magnification had been obtained by lengthening the tube to 100 feet or more, but by combining lenses with mirrors equal magnifying power was achieved within a length of six feet. This was to become the prototype of the instrument to be used for the next 200 years. Two valuable geometrical works followed —the *Vera Quadratus* describing the true quadrature of the circle and hyperbola and the *Geometriae Pars Universalis*. As Regius Professor of Mathematics at the University of St Andrews, Gregory founded the first observatory of its kind in Britain and, as first occupant of the chair of mathematics at the University of Edinburgh, he conducted research which gives him "the right to take his place with Barrow, Newton and Leibniz as a principal discoverer of the differential calculus".[17] These researches were of universal importance but of equal importance was the fact that Gregory was only the first of a distinguished series of Scottish mathematicians.

Natural science also flourished during this period and several Scots were celebrated botanists. Among these was Sir Robert Sibbald who compiled the first natural history of his native land entitled *Scotia Illustrata*. Sibbald and his kinsman Sir Andrew Balfour instituted in 1676 a botanic garden in the grounds of Trinity Hospital, Edinburgh, and it was from their private collections that most of the original plants were procured. The town council willingly gave their support to this scheme and in 1677 the council voted a salary of £20 per year to James Sutherland "a person of knowen abilitie" whom they had selected "for overseeing the culture and for demonstratting the plants . . . considering that this designe will not onlie contribut to the good and ornament of the citie, but also prove exceidinglie profitable for the instruction of youth, in that most necessary, the hitherto much neglected pairt of the naturall historie knowledge, wherein the health of all persones, whether it be for food or medecin, is so nearlie concerned".[18] The educational value of the garden to the medical profession was uppermost in the minds of the founders and in this respect they were fortunate with their first keeper as the fame of the garden was secured with the publication of Sutherland's *Hortus Medicus Edinburgensis* in 1682.

A much more important step, calculated to benefit the medical profession undertaken by the same group of gentlemen who had helped to found the physic garden, was the foundation of the College of Physicians in Edinburgh in 1681. The step had been mooted before but had come to nothing, until in that year a petition for its foundation was presented to the council. Considerable opposition to the new foundation was evident, and the College of Surgeons in particular feared that the new incorporation might infringe its own privileges. But the support of the nobility was gained and the petition was granted on condition that the jurisdiction of the college was

F

restricted to Edinburgh and district; internal diseases were to be treated exclusively by physicians but surgeons alone were to have licence to deal with wounds and accidents; physicians were to have the supervision of drugs and apothecaries' shops, but were not to be exempt from military service. In 1685 three fellows of the new college were appointed by the town council, one of whom Dr Pitcairne was Professor of Medicine at the University of Edinburgh and did much valuable work at home and abroad furthering the cause of medical research. There is no evidence of any of the new fellows delivering lectures at the college, but frequent conferences which anticipated the scientific clubs of the eighteenth century were held to stimulate learning by discussion.

As intellectual attainment increased in at least two of Scotland's major burghs, civic amenities also progressed though sanitary arrangements in the most progressive of burghs remained rudimentary. Both Edinburgh and Glasgow, neither of which expressed strong covenanting tendencies although both had strong presbyterian sympathies, were developing rapidly. Travellers speak enthusiastically about both. Thomas Morer describing Glasgow in 1689 wrote:

Glasgow is a place of great extent and good situation, and has the reputation of the finest town in Scotland, not excepting Edinburgh, though the Royal City. The two main streets are made cross-wise, well paved, and bounded with stately buildings, especially about the centre where they are mostly new, with piazzas under 'em . . . The river is a great current, called the Clyde and conduces much to the riches of the inhabitants, and makes it the most considerable town of that nation. Here are several hospitals . . . and many spires more for ornament than use. And a Tolbooth or Common-hall very magnificent (as most of them are in the towns of Scotland) for public entertainments or city business.[19]

In 1673 hackney coaches were first seen in the streets and five years later the first stage coach between Glasgow and Edinburgh was inaugurated. The coach was to carry six persons, to have six able horses and to make the journey at least once per week, going on Monday and returning on Saturday. Each person was to be allowed one bag and the fare was to be £4.16s. Scots in the summer and £5.8s. in winter. In these towns municipal government was also improving and in Glasgow in 1675, when it was pointed out that non-residents owning property within the city were not liable to bear any of the burgh's burdens, it was enacted that in future each non-resident owner should pay twelve merks annually on every hundred merks of free rental for six preceding years, and the same sum yearly in all time coming. This was the first approach in the city to a systematic levying of rates on the rental value of property.

Equal praise is bestowed upon Edinburgh and most visitors seem to have been struck by the architectural features of the capital. Morer reports that: "Their old houses are cased with boards, and have oval windows without casements or glass which open and shut as stands with their conveniency. Their new houses are made of stone, with good windows modishly framed and glazed, and so lofty that five or six stories is an ordinary height".[20] During this period many public buildings were improved and in 1677 the council enacted that in future houses might not be built or repaired with timber "but aller-narlie with ston work, and they be only thacked with sclait or tyll, under penaltie of fyve hundred merks and demolishing of the buildings".[21] If little real progress towards better social conditions had yet been made an awareness of the problem, even in an age of religious violence and armed insurrection, is clearly evident. The ecclesiastical and political issues arising from the covenants were ever present factors of life in Restoration Scotland but they by no means dominated it. The economic, social and cultural trends which reached their climax in eighteenth-century Scotland all had their roots in a period which far from being the most pitiful in the country's annals has some claim to be regarded as one of the most seminal in the history of the Scottish nation.

BIBLIOGRAPHY

NOTES

INDEX

BIBLIOGRAPHY

The covenants and the Covenanters have always been to the forefront of Scottish historiography but with the exception of quite detailed treatment accorded the subject in some general histories of Scotland such as P. F. Tytler, *History of Scotland*, 9 vols. (Edinburgh: William Tait, 1828–43); J. H. Burton, *History of Scotland*, 9 vols. (Edinburgh: Blackwood, 1873–4); A. Lang, *A History of Scotland*, 4 vols. (Edinburgh: Blackwood, 1900–7); P. H. Brown, *History of Scotland*, 3 vols. (Cambridge: Cambridge University Press, 1908–9) and G. Donaldson, *Scotland: James V to James VII* (Edinburgh: Oliver Boyd, 1965), only two works of reputable scholarship give major attention to the entire covenanting period. These are, W. L. Mathieson, *Politics and Religion: A Study in Scottish History from the Reformation to the Revolution*, 2 vols. (Glasgow: Maclehose & Johnstone, 1902) and J. K. Hewison, *The Covenanters*, 2 vols. (Glasgow: Smith & Son, 1913).

The tendency until the recent publication of D. Stevenson, *The Scottish Revolution, 1637–44: The Triumph of the Covenanters* (Newton Abbot: David & Charles, 1973) had been to concentrate on the later phases of the movement rather than on the years when the covenants commanded widespread support. English historians such as S. R. Gardiner, *History of the Great Civil War*, 3 vols. (London: Longmans, Green & Co., 1886–91) and Dame C. V. Wedgwood, *The King's Peace* (London: Collins, 1955) and *The King's War* (London: Collins, 1958) have further contributed to our knowledge of this period, but in the absence of comparable Scottish works their task was difficult. Understandably their main preoccupation has been with Scottish intervention in England, although on occasions cause and effect in both countries have been successfully interrelated. In this respect two articles by Miss Wedgwood "The Covenanters in the first civil war" in *Scottish Historical Review*, xxxix (1960), 1–15; and "Anglo-Scottish Relations, 1603–40" in *Transactions of the Royal Historical Society*, 4th series, xxxii (1950),

31–48, are particularly successful. On the Scottish side some biographies such as J. Willock, *The Great Marquess: Life and Times of Archibald . . . Marquess of Argyll* (Edinburgh: Oliphant, 1903); M. Napier, *Memoirs of the Marquis of Montrose*, 2 vols. (Edinburgh: Stevenson, 1856); J. Buchan, *Montrose* (London: Nelson, 1928); R. Gilmour, *Samuel Rutherford* (Edinburgh: Oliphant, 1904); R. L. Orr, *Alexander Henderson* (London: Hodder & Stoughton, 1919); J. A. Inglis, *Sir John Hay, "the incendiary"* (Glasgow: Jackson Son & Co., 1937); C. S. Terry, *The Life and Campaigns of Alexander Leslie* (London: Longmans, Green & Co., 1899) and F. N. McCoy, *Robert Baillie and the Second Scots Reformation* (London: University of California Press, 1974), help to illumine the darkness. A few specialist articles are equally useful, but the best of these have been concerned with the "concept of the covenant" rather than with its historical significance. Amongst these may be mentioned S. A. Burrell, "The covenant as a revolutionary symbol—Scotland, 1596–1637" in *Church History*, xxvii (1956), 338–50, the same author's "The apocalyptic vision of the early covenanters" in *Scottish Historical Review*, xliii (1964), 1–24, and G. D. Henderson, "The idea of the covenant in Scotland" in *The Burning Bush* (Edinburgh: The Saint Andrew Press, 1957), 61–74. Hardly surprisingly this dearth of specialist enquiries has been reflected in general histories and goes far to explain the general unanimity of opinion which characterizes all but the most recent survey of the early covenanting period.

Quite the reverse is true of the later phases of the covenanting movement and few historians agree in their interpretation of events after 1660. Their disagreements were also contemporary, for both the Covenanters and their opponents thought fit not only to publish their philosophical judgments in works such as J. Brown, *An Apologetical Relation* (n.p. 1665); [J. Stewart], *Ius Populi Vindicatum* (n.p., 1669) and A. Shields, *A Hind let Loose* (n.p., 1687), but also to interpret their actions in the light of events. In this respect J. Stewart and J. Stirling, *Naphtali, or the Wrestlings of the Church of Scotland* (Glasgow, 1721), first published in 1667, and the "Secret and True history of the Church of Scotland" by James Kirkton (unpublished at the time, but widely circulated) established a tradition which retorts such as A. Honyman, *A Survey of Naphtali* (Edinburgh, 1668–9) and G. MacKenzie, *Ius Regium* (London, 1684) could not effectively counter. This contemporary literature is "extreme, biased, venomous" and requires careful handling,[1] as in the main the Covenanters were more successful in presenting their case than were their opponents, whose replies were further discredited after the establishment of presbyterianism in 1690. In the shadow of this success Gilbert Burnet, *History of his Own Time*, 2 vols. (London, 1724–34) and Robert Wodrow, *The History of the Sufferings of the Church of Scotland from the Restoration to the Revolution*, 2 vols. (Edinburgh, 1721–2; 4 vols., ed. R. Burns, Glasgow 1828–30) established the covenanting tradition. By the mid-eighteenth century, however, the mood had changed. The Erastianism or subordination of the church to the state against which the Covenanters had directed much of their energy was approved by the dominant Moderate party and the ideals of the covenant found little favour with the scholars of that period. Thus when Kirkton's history was eventually published (Edinburgh, 1817) he had the misfortune to find an unsympathetic editor in C. K. Sharpe who could write: "What Kirkton and his associates decerned as, or pretended to think, a noble stand for religion and liberty, can be regarded by an unprejudiced eye in no other light than that of bigotted obstinacy and unprovoked rebellion."[2] However, with the triumph of the Evangelicals and the emergence of the Free Church in the nineteenth century, opinion again swung in favour of the Covenanters, and to this period (which retained its character well into the twentieth century) can be attributed the vast number of hagiographical biographies and "uncritical sentimental panegyrics" on the part of presbyterian historians, only countered in their lack of historicity by the works of episcopalian writers to whom the covenanting movement was "a mere vulgar fanaticism, or at least martyrdom by mistake".[3] Of the many works produced at this time such as: M. Macdonald, *The Covenanters in Moray and Ross* (Inverness: Melven Bros., 1892); J. W. Brown, *The Covenanters of the Merse* (Edinburgh: Oliphant, 1893); P. Walker, *Biographia Presbyteriana*, 2 vols. (Edinburgh: Stevenson, 1827); A Ferguson, *The Laird of Lag* (Edinburgh: David

Douglas, 1886); T. Stephen, *The Life and Times of Archbishop Sharp* (London: Rickerby, 1839); D. Butler, *The Life and Letters of Robert Leighton* (London: Hodder & Stoughton, 1903); and A. J. Mackay, *Memoir of Sir James Dalrymple, first Viscount Stair* (Edinburgh: Edmonston & Douglas, 1873), only the latter can be safely recommended as less biased than others. Mathieson, *Politics and Religion* and Hewison, *The Covenanters*, continue to be the only fairly reliable secondary authorities, although in the later period Mathieson's lack of sympathy with the covenanting cause becomes more apparent, while Hewison's bias in the other direction becomes equally obvious. Of earlier writers the greatest influence in this direction was undoubtedly provided by the seceder Thomas McCrie (Jr.) with works such as his *Life of Alexander Henderson* (Edinburgh, 1846) and *Sketches of Scottish Church History*, 2 vols. (Edinburgh, 1846–9). But while biased in their commentaries, McCrie and other earlier writers frequently quote extensively from original sources, and should not be entirely overlooked. Much of this material has, however, been superseded by the extensive editions of source material which characterized Scottish historical publishing during the nineteenth and early twentieth centuries. (Details of such sources will be found in Stevenson, *The Scottish Revolution*, 381–8, and Donaldson, *James V to James VII*, 416–17, 419.) But not all the papers and documents cited in secondary works are available in printed collections and in this respect even Wodrow, many of whose documents have subsequently appeared in the *Register of the Privy Council*, cannot be entirely disregarded.

In the early twentieth century, the availability of such source material was reflected in the appearance of a number of useful biographies such as C. S. Terry, *John Graham of Claverhouse, Viscount of Dundee* (London: Archibald Constable & Co., 1905); J. Willock, *A Scots Earl of Covenanting Times . . . Archibald, 9th Earl of Argyll* (Edinburgh: Andrew Elliot, 1907); A. Lang, *Sir George MacKenzie* (London: Longmans, Green & Co., 1909); A. Robertson, *The Life of Sir Robert Murray* (London: Longmans, Green & Co., 1922) and W. C. Mackenzie, *Life and Times of John Maitland, Duke of Lauderdale* (London: Kegan Paul, Trench, Trubner & Co., 1923). Of non-biographical studies, C. S. Terry, *The Pentland Rising and Rullion Green* (Glasgow: Maclehose & Sons, 1905) and J. R. Elder, *The Highland Host of 1678* (Aberdeen: Maclehose & Sons, 1914) are valuable studies of particular incidents within the period.

In recent years, if one "peculiarly hysterical attack"[4] on the Covenanters—M. E. M. Donaldson, *Scotland's Suppressed History* (London: John Murray, 1935)—can be discounted, no major work on the subject has appeared although W. R. Foster, *Bishop and Presbytery: the Church of Scotland 1661–1688* (London: SPCK, 1958) is a useful study of ecclesiastical administration. On the other hand two biographies, A. I. Dunlop, *William Carstares and the Kirk by Law Established* (Edinburgh: The Saint Andrews Press, 1967) and A. Veitch *Richard Cameron, the Lion of the Covenant* (London: Pickering & Inglis, 1948) and a number of articles such as J. Bulloch, "Ecclesiastical intolerance in seventeenth-century Berwickshire" in *History of the Berwickshire Naturalists' Club*, xxxvi (1963), 148–58; A. Murray, "Auld Lag and the Covenanters" in *Transactions of Dumfries and Galloway Antiquarian Society*, xxxvi (1959), 149–74; W. F. Bell, "South Perthshire and the covenanting struggle" in *Records of Scottish Church History Society (RSCHS)* i (1926), 71–80; H. Macpherson, "John Blackadder, the Covenanter" in *RSCHS*, iv (1932), 162–75, and "The Wigtown Martyrs" in *RSCHS*, ix (1947), 166–84; D. E. Easson, "A Scottish Parish in covenanting times" in *RSCHS*, x (1950), 141–53; J. A. Lamb, "Archbishop Alexander Burnet, 1614–1684" in *RSCHS*, xi (1952), 133–48; T. Maxwell, "Presbyterian and Episcopalian in 1688" in *RSCHS*, xiii (1957), 23–57, and Julia Buckroyd, "The Dismissal of Archbishop Alexander Burnet, 1669" in *RSCHS*, xviii (1973), 149–55, have helped to advance understanding of the covenanting course. If books such as J. Barr, *The Scottish Covenanters* (Glasgow: Smith & Son, 1946), written in an earlier vein, continue to support popular belief about the Covenanters and their cause, the ultimate corrective lies in the gradual assimilation of these scholarly monographs into the general history of Scotland.

NOTES AND REFERENCES

(The titles of books and articles not cited in full will be found
in the bibliography)

Introduction

1. G. D. Henderson, *Religious Life in Seventeenth-Century Scotland*
(London: Cambridge University Press, 1937), 158

Chapter One   *The Covenants*

1. W. C. Dickinson and G. Donaldson, *A Source Book of Scottish
History*, vol. iii (Edinburgh: Nelson, 1961, hereafter cited as
Source Book), 104
2. Ibid., iii, 101
3. Ibid., iii, 101
4. Mathieson, *Politics and Religion*, i, 381; John, Earl of Rothes,
A Relation of Proceedings concerning the Affairs of the Kirk of Scotland,
ed. D. Laing (Bannatyne Club, 1830), 73
5. J. K. Cameron, *The First Book of Discipline* (Edinburgh: The
Saint Andrew Press, 1972), 200n
6. Donaldson, *James V to James VII*, 322
7. D. Nobbs, *England and Scotland, 1560–1707* (London: Hutchison's University Library, 1952), 99–101
8. *Source Book*, iii, 121
9. Ibid., iii, 122
10. Mathieson, *Politics and Religion*, ii, 63; Lang, *History*, iii, 109;
Donaldson, *James V to James VII*, 331–2
11. *The Letters and Journals of Robert Baillie*, ed. D. Laing, 3 vols.
(Bannatyne Club, 1841–2), ii, 102
12. Wedgwood, "The Covenanters in the first civil war" in *SHR*,
xxxix (1960), 14
13. *Source Book*, iii, 135
14. Brown, *History*, ii, 344–5; Lang, *History*, iii, 192–3
15. Henderson, *Religious Life*, 171
16. *Source Book*, iii, 140–3
17. Ibid., iii, 145
18. Mathieson, *Politics and Religion*, ii, 166
19. Hewison, *Covenanters*, ii, 49; Mathieson, *Politics and Religion*, ii,
171, 175

Chapter Two   The Restoration Settlement

1. *Register of the Consultations of the Ministers of Edinburgh*, ed. W. Stephen, 2 vols. (Scottish History Society, 1921–30), ii, 175
2. Ibid., ii, 160
3. Wodrow, *History of the Sufferings*, i, 5
4. Ibid., i, 4
5. Ibid., i, 6
6. Ibid., i, 7
7. Ibid., i, 18, 20
8. Ibid., i, 18
9. Ibid., i, 9
10. Ibid., i, 10
11. Ibid., i, 28
12. *Lauderdale Papers*, ed. O. Airy, 3 vols. (Camden Society, 1884–5), i, 24
13. Wodrow, *History of the Sufferings*, i, 29–32
14. Ibid., 38; Stephen, *Life of Sharp*, 66–7
15. S. Rutherford, *Lex Rex: The Law and the Prince* . . . (1644)
16. Wodrow, *History of the Sufferings*, i, 45–6
17. Ibid., i, 37–8
18. Ibid., 80–1
19. *Register of the Consultations of the Ministers of Edinburgh*, ii, 221
20. *Source Book*, iii, 155–6
21. Wodrow, *History of the Sufferings*, i, 117–8
22. Sir G. MacKenzie, *Memoirs of the Affairs of Scotland*, ed. Thomson (Edinburgh, 1821), 55–6
23. *Lauderdale Papers*, ii, Appendix C, lxxviii
24. *The Register of the Privy Council of Scotland* (RPC), 3rd series, i–xv, 1660–90 (1908–67), i, 28
25. Ibid., i, 30–2
26. Kirkton, *History*, 127
27. *Lauderdale Papers*, i, 229–30
28. *Source Book*, iii, 159
29. Ibid., iii, 157–8
30. "Jacob Curate", *Scotch Presbyterian Eloquence* (London, 1694), 9

Chapter Three   The Church Divided

1. Burnet, *History of his Own Time*, i, 269
2. Hewison, *Covenanters*, ii, 165
3. Burnet, *History of his Own Time*, i, 264; Donaldson, *James V–James VII*, 367–8

4. *Source Book*, iii, 164–5
5. *Register of the Synod of Galloway, October 1664 to April 1671* (Kirkcudbright, 1856), 52–3
6. *RPC*, 3rd series, ii, 109
7. Hewison, *Covenanters*, ii, 189
8. *Memoirs of Rev. John Blackadder*, ed. A. Crichton (Edinburgh, 1823), 136

Chapter Four   The Pentland Rising

Note: Full details of the Rising and an account of the battle of Rullion Green will be found in C. S. Terry, *The Pentland Rising and Rullion Green* (Glasgow, Maclehose and Son, 1905).

1. *Memoirs of Mr. William Veitch and George Brysson*, ed. T. McCrie (Edinburgh, 1825), 416
2. *Blackadder Memoirs*, 136
3. *Lauderdale Papers*, i, 263, 266
4. Ibid., i, 245
5. *Memoirs of Blackadder*, 137
6. Ibid., 138; Kirkton, *History*, 231; Sir James Turner, *Memoir of his own Life and Times* (Bannatyne Club, 1829), 145
7. Ibid., 145
8. Ibid., 149
9. Ibid., 149
10. *Memoirs of Blackadder*, 138
11. Robert Law, *Memorialls*, ed. C. K. Sharpe (Edinburgh, 1819), 16
12. Turner, *Memoirs*, 157; Terry, *Pentland Rising*, 55
13. *RPC*, 3rd series, ii, 211–12
14. Ibid., ii, 216
15. Turner, *Memoirs*, 176
16. Ibid., 163
17. Ibid., 170
18. Kirkton, *History*, 240
19. Ibid., 232
20. Turner, *Memoirs*, 154
21. Veitch and Bryson, *Memoirs*, 404
22. Ibid., 408
23. *RPC*, 3rd series, ii, 227
24. Ibid., ii, 231
25. Ibid., ii, 241
26. *Lauderdale Papers*, i, 254

27. Ibid., ii, 24
28. Ibid., ii, 11
29. Ibid., ii, App. no. xxxii

Chapter Five   Conciliation

1. W. Row, *Life of Robert Blair* (Wodrow Soc. 1848), 398; Henderson, *Religious Life*, 175
2. Burnet, *History of his Own Time*, i, 499
3. *Lauderdale Papers*, ii, 68
4. Ibid., ii, 121
5. Mathieson, *Politics and Religion*, ii, 234
6. *Lauderdale Papers*, ii, 139
7. *Source Book*, iii, 160
8. *Lauderdale Papers*, ii, lxviii
9. Mathieson, *Politics and Religion*, ii, 247 and n
10. *Source Book*, iii, 171—2

Chapter Six   Renewed Repression

1. Hewison, *Covenanters*, ii, 233
2. *RPC*, 3rd series, iv, 296
3. Ibid., iv, 358
4. Ibid., iv, 381–2
5. Ibid., iv, 386
6. Carrington Kirk Session Records cited D. E. Easson, "A Scottish Parish in Covenanting Times" in *Records of Scottish Church History Society*, ix, 116
7. Ibid., ix, 118
8. *RPC*, 3rd series, iv, 462–3
9. Ibid., 3rd series, v, 198
10. Hewison, *Covenanters*, ii, 257
11. *RPC*, 3rd series, iv, 664
12. Burnet, *History of his Own Time*, ii, 141
13. Mathieson, *Politics and Religion*, ii, 271–2
14. Wodrow, *History of the Sufferings*, iii, 37–8
15. Hackston held back and refused to take an active part in Sharp's murder, but may be deemed as an accessory (Ibid., iii, 42–4)
16. Ibid., iii, 66–7
17. *Memoirs of Blackadder*, 220
18. Wodrow, *History of the Sufferings*, iii, 104
19. Hewison, *Covenanters*, ii, 306

20. Burnet, *History of his Own Time*, ii, 240. The gibbet and the cart-load of ropes for the hanging of prisoners taken by the Covenanters have been the cause of much dispute. The gibbet, however, was the public gibbet of the nether ward of Lanark and the ropes lack authentication. Lang, *History*, iii, 352–3 and Hewison, *Covenanters*, ii, 312n disagree on this issue. "The Bluidie Banner" (Lang, *History*, iii, 352 and n) does seem to be of later manufacture (W. McMillan, "The Covenanters after the Revolution of 1688", *RSCHS*, x [1950], 141–4)

21. *RPC*, 3rd series, vi, 257, 263

Chapter Seven   The Aftermath, Cameronians and Presbyterians

1. *Source Book*, iii, 175–7
2. Ibid., iii, 177–9
3. Wodrow, *History of the Sufferings*, iii, 350–3
4. Scots Confession of Faith in *John Knox's History of the Reformation in Scotland*, 2 vols. (Edinburgh: Nelson, 1949), ii, 262, 264
5. *RPC*, 3rd series, vii, 239
6. *Source Book*, iii, 186–9; *RPC*, 3rd series, vii, 239
7. Donaldson, *James V to James VII*, 371
8. *RPC*, 3rd series, vii, 242
9. Hewison, *Covenanters*, ii, 371
10. *Reports of the Royal Commission on Historical Manuscripts* (London, 1870–   ), xv, part viii, 271
11. *RPC*, 3rd series, vii, 384
12. *Melrose Regality Records*, ed. C. S. Romanes, 3 vols. (Scottish History Society, 1914–17), iii, 24
13. Ibid., iii, 32
14. Wodrow, *History of the Sufferings*, iii, 409
15. *RPC*, 3rd series, vii, 431–2
16. Ibid., 3rd series, viii, 108
17. Hewison, *Covenanters*, ii, 400
18. Ibid., ii, 400
19. Ibid., ii, 401
20. Ibid., ii, 406
21. *RPC*, 3rd series, viii, 318–19
22. *Historical Manuscripts Commission*, xv, part viii, 287
23. *RPC*, 3rd series, ix, 80

Chapter Eight   The Killing Times

1. *RPC*, 3rd series, ix, 159
2. *Source Book*, iii, 181–2

3. Hewison, *Covenanters*, ii, 446–7
4. A. Shields, *The Life and Death of . . . J. Renwick* (Edinburgh, 1724), 52–3
5. *RPC*, 3rd series, x, 37
6. Ibid., 3rd series, xi, 70
7. Ibid., 3rd series, x, 84
8. Ibid., 3rd series, x, 85
9. Ibid., 3rd series, xi, 26
10. Hewison, *Covenanters*, ii, 473
11. *RPC*, 3rd series, x, 107
12. See M. Napier, *The Case for the Crown in re the Wigtown Martyrs* (Edinburgh, 1863); *History Rescued, in Answer to "History Vindicated"* (Edinburgh, 1870); A. Stewart, *History Vindicated in the Case of the Wigtown Martyrs* (Edinburgh, 1867)
13. H. Macpherson, "The Wigtown Martyrs" in *Records of Scottish Church History Society*, ix, 183
14. Ibid., 174
15. *Historical Manuscripts Comm.*, xv, part viii, 146
16. Wodrow, *History of the Sufferings*, iv, 262
17. Hewison, *Covenanters*, ii, 488
18. *Source Book*, iii, 182–4
19. Ibid., iii, 194
20. *RPC*, 3rd series, xii, 435
21. *Source Book*, iii, 196
22. Ibid., iii, 196
23. Ibid., iii, 197
24. Wodrow, *History of the Sufferings*, iv, 432

Chapter Nine   The Triumph of Presbyterianism

1. T. Maxwell, "Presbyterian and Episcopalian in 1688" in *Records of Scottish Church History Society*, xiii, 28
2. *Acts of the Parliaments of Scotland (APS)*, edd. T. Thomson and C. Innes, 12 vols. (Edinburgh 1814–75), ix, 17
3. *Source Book*, iii, 205
4. Ibid., iii, 207
5. Wodrow, *History of the Sufferings*, iv, 435–6
6. R. Keith, *An Historical Catalogue of the Scottish Bishops* (Edinburgh, 1824), 69
7. Ibid., 69
8. *Source Book*, iii, 212
9. Ibid, iii, 212

10. J. Cunningham, *Church History of Scotland*, 2 vols. (Edinburgh, 1882), ii, 201–2

11. T. Stephen, *History of the Church of Scotland*, 4 vols. (London, 1844), iii, 650

12. Hewison, *Covenanters*, ii, 524

13. M. Shields, *Faithful Contendings Displayed*, ed. J. Howie (Edinburgh, 1780), 393–404

14. W. McMillan, "The Covenanters after the Revolution of 1688" in *Records of Scottish Church History Society*, x, 144

15. Auchensaugh Declaration cited in W. Ferguson, *Scotland 1689 to the Present* (Edinburgh: Oliver & Boyd, 1968), 112

16. McMillan, "Covenanters after the Revolution" in *RSCHS*, x, 145

Chapter Ten   Post-Restoration Scotland

1. Brown, *History*, ii, 379

2. *APS*, vii, 8

3. Ibid., vii, 255

4. Ibid., vii, 256

5. Ibid., vii, 652

6. Ibid., viii, 348; *RPC*, 3rd series, vii, 43

7. *Records of Convention of Royal Burghs of Scotland*, ed. J. D. Marwick, 6 vols. (Edinburgh, 1866–90), iii, 523

8. R. Chambers, *Domestic Annals of Scotland*, 3 vols. (Edinburgh: W. & R. Chambers, 1858–61), ii, 398

9. *RPC*, 3rd series, viii, 241–2

10. G. P. Insh, *Scottish Colonial Schemes*, 1620–86 (Glasgow: Maclehose, Jackson & Co., 1922), 123

11. *RPC*, 3rd series, vii, 665

12. Insh, *Scottish Colonial Schemes*, 118

13. *RPC*, 3rd series, vii, 664

14. Sir Walter Scott, "Wandering Willies Tale", in *Redgauntlet* (Border edition, London: Nimmo, 1894), i, 165

15. J. Dryden, "Discourse concerning Satire", in *Poems of John Dryden*, ed. J. Kinsley, 4 vols. (Oxford: Clarendon Press, 1958), ii, 666

16. Sir G. MacKenzie, *Ius Regium* (London, 1684), 51

17. James Gregory *Tercentenary Memorial Volume*, ed. H. W. Turnbull (St Andrews: Royal Society of Edinburgh, 1939), 13

18. Edinburgh Town Council Register, vol. xxviii, fo. 215 cited in *Scottish Historical Review*, xii, 375

19. A. M. MacKenzie, *Scottish Pageant*, 1625–1707 (Edinburgh: Oliver & Boyd, 1949), 12
20. Ibid., 11
21. Edinburgh Town Council Register, vol. xxviii, fos. 123–4 cited in *Scottish Historical Review*, xii, 374

Bibliography

1. Henderson, *Religious Life*, 158
2. Kirkton, *History*, viii
3. Henderson, *Religious Life*, 158
4. Ibid., 158

INDEX